LEVERAGING UP

Leveraging UP

Mastering the 8 Universal Principles for Success in Your Leadership Journey

Dr. Debora Trimpe

Published by Game Changer Publishing

Paperback ISBN: 978-1-965653-78-4

Hardcover ISBN: 978-1-965653-79-1

Digital ISBN: 978-1-965653-80-7

GC GAME CHANGER
PUBLISHING
www.GameChangerPublishing.com

DEDICATION

I dedicate this book to all those leaders who have taught me so much about effective leadership. Aaron Graham and Tony Marchbanks, you are truly two of the best leaders I have ever worked with, exemplifying the very meaning of transformational leadership. Thank you for your mentorship. I also want to thank the leaders of the Dallas HBA for allowing me to lead that organization as their first woman president. It was an honor to have the opportunity to learn how to lead through influence and not through title. Last, I want to thank my husband, Steve, for his support and understanding as I continue to take on these new challenges in my life and my daughter, Heidi, for all the help and support she has provided me and our business so that I have the opportunity to take on these varied challenges.

READ THIS FIRST

Just to say thanks for buying and reading my book, I would like to give you a free bonus gift, no strings attached!

Scan the QR Code Here:

LEVERAGING UP

MASTERING THE 8 UNIVERSAL PRINCIPLES
FOR SUCCESS IN YOUR LEADERSHIP JOURNEY

DR. DEBORA TRIMPE

GC GAME CHANGER
PUBLISHING
www.GameChangerPublishing.com

CONTENTS

INTRODUCTION

I have over 45 years of experience in the business world. And when I say experience, I don't just mean working in a business—I also mean the experience of hard knocks in business. I have held positions ranging from receptionist to owning my own home-building company for 10 years. Now, I am a consultant and own my current practice as well.

I wanted to write this book because something compelled me to make a change. In 2020, I wrote a book called *No Room for Failure*, which was focused on sales, specifically real estate and new home sales. While that book was interesting and helpful, and although I achieved great results for the people I worked with, I began to feel a little stale. I became a little bored. Why? Because I felt like I wasn't helping as many people as I could.

Certainly, if I helped someone with their sales, it benefited them: they made more money, became more successful, and this positively affected their families and possibly even their friends. However, while I could help those individuals, I wondered what if I could help so many more.

I have worked in training, managerial, and leadership roles. I started to ask myself, *What if I could find a better way for people who lead? If I could provide a framework and principles that could guide their lives, how much more impact could I have on them and the worlds around them?* By influencing the leader, I would also impact their families, their employees, and, certainly, the businesses they work for.

In 2009, I was the director of training for a large, privately held home-building company. During that time, we were going through the Great Recession, which began in 2008. In 2009, as I coached and talked with people, I encountered many who were completely despondent. I had men sitting in front of me crying, because they were no longer able to earn the money they once did.

In that situation, I decided I needed more education so I could better help these people. That's why I went back to school and earned my master's degree in leadership coaching psychology, followed by a PhD in industrial and organizational psychology. What is that, you ask? Essentially, it's psychology for the workplace. It covers topics such as goal-setting, motivation, hiring, negotiation—everything we deal with in the workplace. So, beyond my years of business experience and my desire to make a difference, I have blended my experience, passion, and education to create this book.

Now, why did I write this book? Well, as I mentioned, I spent many years coaching in sales, watching people grow and succeed. Yet, much of their growth and success was hampered by their managers. I probably felt some guilt about that. My first job as a sales manager came after winning a contest! You read that right. I believed I had the abilities to lead and could be good at it, but my first boss taught me many leadership lessons—though not necessarily in a good way. As I grew and met others in leadership, I found that many had the same experience I did: little to no preparation for leadership roles. Their companies had not invested the time, energy, or money in developing leaders at all levels. I realized many leaders shared the same struggles, and I asked myself, *How could I help them?* I felt this book could offer some answers.

Finally, there is the faith-based aspect of this conversation. You may believe in a higher power, whether you call it God or something else. Or perhaps you've had bad experiences with religion and have sworn off anything faith-based. I totally understand. But in my conversations with most people, we generally agree that there is some universal strength or power greater than all of us. If we can tap into the principles and values of that universal source, it can dramatically change our lives. It is the true compass.

As you read this book, you will see that I have devoted a chapter to each of the **8 Universal Principles** I believe are some of the most valuable in becoming the most successful leader. Each of these chapters provides background information about what each of the Universal Principles means and offers a thorough description of how you can utilize these principles as a leader. You'll find examples of how others have used these principles and the impact they've had not only on the leaders but also on those they lead.

For ease of use, I have also written this book in a way that does not require you to use each chapter in the order in which they are presented. You are welcome to go to the chapter that seems most likely to discuss the issue you are most interested in. You can utilize the strategies there. However, I would suggest that implementing one principle without the others will not get you the best results over time.

ONE

THE UNIVERSAL PRINCIPLE
OF ABUNDANCE

Now, I know that when many of you think about the word "abundance," you might immediately associate it with the law of attraction. This is understandable, given the influence of media and popular culture. But I want to step back for a minute and ask you to consider the real definition of abundance. It's about plentifulness—the ability to have plenty, right? Now, that could mean money. But why not joy, fulfillment, or success? Abundance can take many forms.

The first concept I want you to grasp from this chapter is to think of abundance as "plenty." Detach it from money, success, and growth for a moment, and just think about what "plentiful" means to you, personally. If you do that, everything in this chapter will make much more sense. The **Universal Principle of Abundance** teaches us that whatever we want to achieve, we can receive.

Let me repeat that for you: Whatever we want to achieve, we can receive. You may be thinking, "I've heard this before." Or perhaps you've read it in books like Napoleon Hill's *Think and Grow*

Rich!,[1] one of the most famous self-help books ever written. Hill was a man ahead of his time. Or maybe you've come across similar ideas in the works of Tony Robbins. Their shared perspective is that we can achieve whatever we set our minds to. And a lot of it, of course, has to do with mindset.

Whatever we set our minds to, we can achieve. So, the first part of applying the Universal Principle of Abundance is having the right mindset—accepting the idea that what we believe can affect what happens in our lives. But here's something important: Mindset isn't necessarily about what you believe.

You see, the problem with beliefs is that they are convictions, definitions we accept as true. And people often say it takes three to four weeks to change a belief. Well, they're wrong. Here's a key point: If you've ever failed at a diet, exercise plan, or anything you wanted to change, it's because no one told you that it takes 63 days to form a new neural pathway. That's right—it takes about two months to change a belief because that's how long it takes to rewire your brain.

What we're going to discuss here is an energy-saving shortcut to understanding the world. And that shortcut is your perspective. We'll explore this more in a later chapter, but for now, let's focus on perspective.

Perspective is how you see something. So, instead of focusing on a belief, let's shift to the perspective that there is plenty out there —that whatever I truly desire in my life is available to me. And if I accept the perspective that I am the only one standing in my way, how much could my life change? Well, that's great, you might say; you've told me all about abundance and growing rich, but how does this apply to leadership? Here's how.

In leadership, as in life, people often come from a place of scarcity. If you've ever read any of the books by Robert Cialdini, especially his brilliant book *Influence,* you know that people are

---

1. Hill, N. (1937). *Think and Grow Rich!*

more motivated by the fear of loss than by the potential for gain. We, as humans, are wired to focus on the negative. Our brains are hardwired for survival, so anything bad that happens sticks to us like Velcro, while good experiences slide off like Teflon. We hang onto the negative because we want to avoid repeating painful situations. The good? Well, if it happens again, great—but it doesn't stick with us in the same way.

Now, think about that.

If we are wired to believe in scarcity—the opposite of abundance—and we are motivated by the fear of loss more than the benefit of gain, can you understand why the Principle of Abundance is so hard for many people to incorporate into their lives?

So what do we do? We live in fear and distress about everything going wrong. We do it every day. But what if we decided to change our perspective? What if we decided to believe that anything we want is already there? I assure you, if you adopted that perspective, your life would change immeasurably. If you begin to see abundance as something that already exists—that you can access what you need when you need it—your reactions to situations, purposes, and even people will shift. Imagine believing that whatever you're looking for, you can absolutely find. That's where the Universal Principle of Abundance comes in. It teaches that whatever we want is already there, so let's start looking for what's already available.

I know that sounds way simpler than it is. But if everything you've ever wanted, or will want, is already available to you, what will you do to get it? For me, the Universal Principle of Abundance is very much like a self-fulfilling prophecy. Everything is going to go great. I can find a solution to any problem. Whatever resource I need is out there—I just need to look harder to find it.

When you meet a person who embraces this principle, what do their lives look like? Sad and empty? Of course not. Things seem to go well for them. You know, those people who just seem inherently lucky? Well, they're not really lucky—they just expect good things to happen, and they do.

You need to understand that the self-fulfilling prophecy is a mirror of your thinking. If you believe everything is negative, then you're going to get negative results. To get positive results, the self-fulfilling prophecy needs to align with the thought that you are going to have good results and that plentiful resources are available to you. So, let's apply this to your leadership style. Where do we see abundance issues coming up? So many people I work with say things like, "I just can't find good people," or "I can't find people willing to show up and work," or "We can't get this project done—there's just not enough time." Others say, "My bosses don't get it—they won't give me the resources I need." Sound familiar? Of course it does. We've all said these things.

And how does that reflect in your employees? You might hear things like, "This is way too much to do," or "I can't find any work-life balance in this company." Some may fear layoffs: "Others are getting laid off—what about me? Am I next?" or "I can't do this job because I don't have [fill in the blank]." Another common refrain: "I'm not getting paid enough to do what you're asking me to do."

All of these thoughts reflect how the Universal Principle of Abundance is being misused. How can that be? We're not using it the right way—we're getting plenty of results we *don't* want. So let's say we want to apply the Universal Principle of Abundance in a way that benefits us. How do we do that?

First, as I mentioned earlier, we need to act in harmony with abundance, not scarcity. Remember, our "caveman brain" constantly thinks bad things are going to happen. And as Robert Cialdini says, we are motivated by scarcity, not by the hope of better things.

So, the first step in applying the Universal Principle of Abundance is to be aware of our thoughts. We need to be vigilant about them. When leading others, we must view every situation as an opportunity, rather than as bad luck or a negative consequence.

Think about that.

So many times, when something negative happens, we chalk it up to "bad luck." But there's no such thing as bad luck. It's all about how we choose to perceive and handle situations, right?

Let's get back to acting in harmony with abundance and see what we can achieve. I'll give you an example of a leader I worked with, whom I'll call Annie for the purposes of this book. (All identities will be withheld to protect the good, the innocent, and the naive.) Annie came to me and said, "I just cannot find the right people. I can't seem to hire anyone. I'm getting resumes, but none of them meet the job requirements. None of the people I'm interviewing are the caliber of candidates I want to hire. There's just no one out there."

Now, when we think about this situation and how it relates to the Universal Principle of Abundance, are we thinking in terms of abundance or scarcity? Obviously, it's scarcity. So, the first thing I did with Annie was to help her shift her mindset. Instead of thinking every day that "there's no one out there," we worked on assuming that there *were* lots of good people out there—they just weren't aware of her company.

Maybe the job description wasn't effectively promoting what she was really looking for. When we hold a mindset or belief that we can't find the right people, we act in accordance with that belief. So, if that's your starting point—"I can't find the right people"— can you see how you might not be putting your best message out there? Maybe relying solely on automated platforms to post jobs isn't the best way, in all situations, to find the right person. Maybe you should be looking elsewhere. If you believe the right person is out there, what might you do? You'd turn over every stone and leave nothing unexamined. And yet, I watch leaders use only one platform to advertise jobs.

What about referrals? What about going to your existing employees, especially the ones you really like? Tell them, "I love your attitude, your work performance, and your daily commitment. Who do you know who's just like you—someone you'd enjoy working with?" Have you thought about that? Annie hadn't.

Then we discussed the job description she posted. It was so bland and lacking in color that it's hard to imagine anyone wanting to apply, unless they were desperate for a job. And that's exactly the kind of candidates she was getting. So, we had Annie refine her job description, adding elements that would attract the kinds of people she wanted to hire. She started incorporating language that highlighted the opportunity to positively influence the workplace environment, which was how she wanted her new employee to view their role.

If you want someone who works hard, is motivated to change, and is driven by positive behavior, then that's the kind of environment they want to work in. So, we started adding more details to the job posting that highlighted challenges because Annie wanted someone who loved challenges and would work to find solutions.

Now, what we did was begin to act in harmony with the Universal Principle of Abundance. We embraced the idea that there were, in fact, many people out there who were exactly what Annie needed. Once she adopted the perspective that these people existed, and she began to internalize that mindset, things started to happen. Notice that we didn't try to change her beliefs—according to researcher Joe Dispenza, that would take at least 63 days, and we didn't have that kind of time to hire someone. Instead, we shifted her perspective from "There's no one out there for this job" to "There are plenty of people out there who want this job."

We changed Annie's perspective from believing she had used all available job-posting platforms to realizing that perhaps she hadn't used the right platforms or described the job effectively to attract the candidates she was seeking. Within just a few days of changing how she was searching for candidates and revising the job description, Annie had over ten highly qualified candidates for the position.

In fact, she told me, "It's almost impossible to make a choice;

they're all so good." She hired one of them, who has since been a phenomenal employee and has done great things for her company. Later, Annie even went back and reached out to two of the other candidates she hadn't hired for the first position and brought them on for other roles. There was such a strong connection between her and these candidates in terms of their thinking, beliefs, and how they viewed the work environment and job fulfillment. Many of them told her that they would love to know if any other positions opened up because they really wanted to work with her.

Now, let's also consider what happens in the workplace when something goes wrong. I'd like to share a story about someone you may or may not have heard of—Vishen Lakhiani, the founder and CEO of Mindvalley. In a program I watched recently, Vishen said that so many people, when faced with challenges, ask, "Why is this happening to me?" instead of, "Why is this happening for me?"

What Vishen said aligns perfectly with the Universal Principle of Abundance. When we ask, "Why is this happening to me?" we're coming from a place of scarcity and lack. But if we ask, "Why is this happening for me?" we begin to see abundance all around us.

As a leader, you can teach the people you lead to shift their perspective. Instead of wondering why things are happening to them, encourage them to ask, "Why is this happening for me?" What can they learn from it? How can it propel them toward better results? When we start looking at life that way and leading others in that direction, everything changes.

I learned this lesson the hard way in my own career. My boss, who promoted me to my first sales manager position, was the teacher—though I doubt he intended to teach me what I ultimately learned! I'll tell you more about that story later, because it was both the best and worst time in my career as I learned how to be a manager and a leader.

I attended a meeting with ten other people who held director-level positions like mine. My boss—let's call him Darren—loved to ask questions he thought people wouldn't know the answers to, only to mock them in front of everyone. One day, it was my turn. I had been managing 36 salespeople in 18 different locations for about five months when Darren asked me why a specific directional sign at one location wasn't up. I didn't know, and my face gave it away. Darren said, "You didn't know it wasn't up, did you?" I admitted that I didn't. He then berated me for not being a good leader, saying, "Good leaders know these kinds of things."

That moment was a turning point in my career. I promised myself I would never let something like that happen again. I committed to knowing everything Darren might know that I didn't. From that day forward, I worked seven days a week, taking time off only during vacations; for the remaining seven years, I worked for Darren. I never wanted to be in that situation again. More importantly, I never wanted to be seen as an ineffective leader.

So, what did I learn from this, and how does it apply to the Universal Principle of Abundance? What I ultimately understood is that abundance is everywhere. Every experience offers an opportunity to learn and grow. By recognizing the abundance around me, I realized I could take every experience—good or bad—and use it to become my best self.

Although I didn't need to work seven days a week for seven years, I learned that there was something in that experience *for me*. I became a much better leader because I didn't view that situation as something going against me. I saw it as an opportunity to grow and become the best version of myself. I learned that every experience, no matter how challenging, could be used to propel me forward.

Another thing I want you to think about in leadership, especially related to the Universal Principle of Abundance, is that you need to lead from a place of service to others.

I know there's a lot of information out there about servant leadership, and quite frankly, I'm up to my eyeballs in reading about it and what it really means. But let me clarify: Being a servant leader does not mean never asking anyone to do something you wouldn't do yourself.

I'd call that martyrdom. I know many leaders who say, "I'm in the office at 5:30 a.m. I don't leave until 8 p.m. I'm just asking my team to show up on time. I'm doing way more than them, and they still won't do it."

That's not abundance.

That's not positive.

That's all about scarcity—scarcity of time and scarcity of vision. When you work in service, and by that, I mean genuinely giving to others and recognizing the abundance of what you have to offer, the Universal Principle of Abundance says you'll receive in return.

However, the key point is that you don't give with the expectation of receiving something in return. You do it because you know it's the right thing to do. If you want to explore this concept further, I recommend *The Go-Giver* by Bob Burg and John David Mann. It's written in a story format and is easy to digest. The book's premise is that giving and adding value to others leads to greater personal success and fulfillment.

Living the Universal Principle of Abundance requires us to shift from selfishness to selflessness. The more selfless you become in service to others, the greater the return you'll see. Abundance only happens when you give.

Consider the example of a full cup. If you never drink from the cup but keep adding liquid, eventually, the cup will overflow, and the liquid will be wasted. The same happens with abundance. If you keep it all to yourself, the overflow becomes wasted, and you can no longer accept or filter in anything new.

As I mentioned before with Annie, I see a lack of understanding of the Universal Principle of Abundance, especially when it comes to hiring. What do we do? We take what we can get. But, as I said in Annie's example, we should be open-minded and think, "Maybe this person isn't the perfect candidate for this role, but maybe they're perfect for another role." What about referrals? What about those who already understand and appreciate how you lead and enjoy the work environment? What if they could help you reach your goals? We can experience abundance in fortunate events or in unfortunate ones. But I assure you, there's always an answer if we are open enough to find it or receive it.

I suggest that, after reading this chapter, you take some time and, in the space below, list some of the limiting perspectives you have about abundance in your life. It's important to know where you're coming from.

Then, write down what you could do differently to lead in accordance with the positive Universal Principles of Abundance. By doing this and creating an action plan for yourself, you will achieve better results than if you simply read the book, think *That's interesting*, and put it aside. Without action—which is another universal principle we'll discuss later—nothing becomes reality.

ACTION PLAN

Limiting Perspectives

_____

_____

_____

_____

_____

Changes I will make to be in accordance with the Universal Principle of Abundance

_____

_____

_____

_____

_____

TWO

THE UNIVERSAL PRINCIPLE OF ALIGNMENT

So, what does alignment mean to you? If I use a car analogy, you'd likely say that if the car is giving you a bumpy ride, you might think the tires are not in alignment. If our car's tires aren't aligned, what happens? The tire treads wear unevenly, and the car rides roughly. So, we all know what alignment means in terms of a car.

Now, let's consider alignment as it applies to our relationships with people. Have you ever had a conversation with someone and thought, *Oh my gosh, I don't know how this happened, but we connected so easily?* Where the moon, the sun, and the stars just align? Everything flows effortlessly when things are in alignment.

So, when we think about alignment, it's really about the positioning of things in relation to one another. Let me repeat that: It's the positioning of things in relation to one another. Now, the traditional definition of alignment says that strategies, goals, and actions need to be consistent with the overarching objectives or values of the organization. But this is where I want to turn things on their head. The **Universal Principle of Alignment** isn't about ensuring that the people who work with you have their strategies, goals, and actions aligned with the company's objectives—it's actually the reverse. The company needs to understand people's goals, strategies, and actions so it can align with them.

I'm sure some of you are confused. You may be thinking, *Why would we change the objectives of our company to match the goals of the people who work here?* That's not exactly what I'm saying. I've seen leaders come in year after year, especially in sales, and tell people, "This is what we need from you. These are the sales goals we need." And in all the years I've managed and led salespeople, what do you think the most common reaction was?

When we didn't hit the goals—which happened often—the first thing the employee would say was, "I could have told you we were never going to hit those goals." They had a variety of reasons: the goal was too ambitious, prices were too high, competition was too fierce. I heard it all. When you want to be in alignment with your team, ownership is everything. So how do you achieve that alignment if you're not the one setting the goals?

If you're asking that question, you're coming from the wrong perspective. Most leaders think, *If I'm true to myself, then these people have to understand me, work with me, and work toward the goals I set.* That's the misconception of authentic leadership, which is a whole other conversation.

The philosophy I've adopted, after all my work in psychology, is called transformational leadership. That sounds great, right? The ability to lead people and transform them. But how do we do that? This is why I love the concept of transformational leadership—it's perfectly in sync with the Universal Principle of Alignment. What it says is that I need to lead people according to their needs and skills.

How do we define "need?" In this case, it's related to an individual's personality style. Everyone has a different personality. While you already know that, how many of you actually work with people differently based on their personality style? In fact, when I work with leaders who have kids, I ask if they treat all their kids the same in terms of motivation or accountability. They always say "No." Then I ask them the follow-up question: Why not? Why don't you treat them all the same? Their answer is always the same: "They have different personalities." So my question is, why wouldn't you apply that same thinking at work? Why would you treat your family members, whom you love and want to succeed, differently than the people you lead at work? Why would you do less for your work family?

You don't say to your kids, "I'm the parent; this is how I parent, and you better like it." Maybe some people do, I don't know. But most people I know are very aware of their children's personalities. They know what motivates and demotivates them, and they create the right environment for them to succeed. Parents today even know what diets their kids need because not all kids can eat the same things.

So, where's the disconnect between home life and work life? You probably spend more time at work than you do with your family, and yet we often take a completely different approach to those we lead at work. Why don't we treat our employees like our family? So many leaders take the approach, "This is how I lead, fall in step." You're catering to *your* personality needs, not those of the people you lead.

We must understand what our employees need from us emotionally. Some of your team members may need a lot of affirmation. Now, for those of you who don't need affirmation, I know that can drive you crazy. Many of the leaders I work with say, "Deb, I don't need this kind of affirmation. Do I really have to give it to these people?" The answer is yes, of course you do, because that's what motivates them. That's what makes them want to walk through walls for you.

And then there are other people we work with who have that driver personality. All they want is to be acknowledged for what they've given up and the time and effort they've put into contributing to the company as a whole. They don't want to be told every day, "Oh, I couldn't live without you." That's almost cringe-worthy to them. Yet, they also need something from you.

One of the easiest ways to understand personality styles that I recommend is the DISC profile. If you've never seen it, DISC is a personality profiling system that assesses people based on **four basic personality types**. While we all have a combination of these four styles, certain styles will stand out more than others. The styles are: **D for Dominant, I for Influential, S for Steady, and C for Conscientious**. A great resource that makes DISC easy to understand and use is the book *Taking Flight* by Merrick Rosenberg and Daniel Silvert.[1] Now, I'm not going to spend time here explaining the personality profiles in detail—that's something you can explore on your own, and there's plenty of material available. My point is that it's crucial to understand the personality profile of the person you're leading. They need something from you, and it's your responsibility to give it to them.

The second aspect of this conversation relates to how you lead based on the skills of the employee. Would you lead everyone the same way regardless of their skill set? Of course not. If someone has only been in the organization for a week, you wouldn't treat them the same way or have the same expectations as you would for someone who's been with the company for 10 years, right? And yet, leaders often lead their teams as if everyone has the same level of proficiency. That's not very effective, is it?

What we need to do is lead each individual on our team based on their needs and abilities. When you do that, people feel empowered and inspired—something many leaders struggle with. Empowerment allows team members to feel like they have a say in what happens, that their decisions matter. When a team feels empowered, they're more inspired and engaged. Isn't that what we're always striving for?

---

1. Rosenberg, M., Silvert, D. (2015). *Taking Flight!: Master the DISC Styles to Transform Your Career, Your Relationships... Your Life*. Financial Times Pren Hall.

So the first step to achieving alignment, as you can now see, is understanding your employees' personalities—what they need from you emotionally or in terms of attention—and considering their skill levels. If you don't do this, you can't possibly be in alignment with your team. If you take the approach that you lead the way you lead and expect everyone to perform the same way, you'll end up with a dysfunctional team. You'll have employees who aren't empowered, aren't inspired, and don't enjoy working with you. In the Universal Principle of Alignment, you need to understand that *everything*—and I mean *everything*—is connected.

Even science shows us this connection. For example, I remember an experiment I did back in junior high school. I wanted to see what effect music might have on plant growth. I found that plants exposed to rock music twice a day grew only half as much as those "listening" to classical music like Mozart or Beethoven. The difference in growth was obvious.

What does this have to do with alignment? I'm talking about connection. Even plants are connected to the energy of music. Dr. Masaru Emoto conducted a study where he exposed water to different words, music, and spoken intentions before freezing it. The water crystals formed beautifully and symmetrically when exposed to positive words or intentions, but they became distorted and unattractive when exposed to negative ones. This study shows that everything is connected. If something as simple as words can affect water crystallization, imagine what they can do to human beings!

So, if you're not willing to change how you lead by considering personality and ability, you won't be in alignment with the people you lead. Let's talk about what alignment looks like from a leadership perspective.

How do you get in alignment? The first thing I work on with my leadership clients is goal-setting. Now, this is a very misunderstood concept because most companies approach goal-setting by saying, "Here are our goals. This is what you need to do to help us achieve *our* goals."

I've read articles that suggest if you have a mission statement and explain how employees' work contributes to the greater good, they'll be more likely to be in alignment. That's true to an extent. Many Millennials and Zoomers want to feel that what they do has an impact on others. That's great, but it only addresses the needs of some, not all.

It still doesn't get down to what the individual employee's goals are. When I was director of training, I was fortunate enough to have leadership that allowed me to apply concepts I had studied during my master's and doctoral programs.

Much of what I learned about the power of goal-setting came from the research of Edwin Locke and Gary Latham, who were pioneers in this field. If you want to dive deeper, I recommend reading their book, *A Theory of Goal Setting*. This work clearly shows the relationship between goal-setting, performance, and motivation.

Our goal-setting experiment began with a question I asked leadership during a business planning session. I asked, "What percentage of the time are we actually hitting or exceeding our sales goals?" The unfortunate answer was only 47%. That stunned me, and clearly, that's not a number that's going to help a company grow.

I suggested to my leadership team that we change the way we were setting goals for the sales team. Instead of having a meeting and telling the team what sales numbers we expected each month, my strategy was to find out what goals each salesperson wanted to achieve. After explaining the plan in depth and outlining how we would implement it, I made the case that my process would produce different results. Based on everything I had learned, I believed we would see better results. I asked if we could give this plan a try.

They agreed to give me the opportunity, allowing me to have goal-setting conversations with all of the salespeople. I'll walk you through what those conversations looked like in a moment, but first, let me tell you the end result. At the end of that year, we reviewed the numbers, and we had met or exceeded the business plan 86% of the time. Instead of focusing on what the company needed, we focused on what the employee needed. That shift in conversation nearly doubled our results! The clients I've taught this process to have also seen similar outcomes.

So, what does a goal-setting conversation look like? When I sit down with someone—let's say a salesperson, for lack of a better example—the first thing I ask is, "What are *your* sales goals?"

If they say they want to sell 100 units this year or reach $5 million in sales, the typical reaction I see from leaders is to reject the goal if it seems high. They often suggest a lower goal. When asked why, the leader will usually say they thought the goal was unrealistic because the individual didn't come close to that number the previous year.

The first mistake we make is squashing their goal. That's the wrong approach. It's *their* goal. Instead of rejecting it, I ask more questions about what they plan to do differently to reach a goal that's significantly higher than their prior performance. Sometimes they have a clear plan, and sometimes they don't. But let's not worry about that right now.

The second question I ask is, "If you were to reach this goal, what would that do for you?" In sales, they'll likely mention making more money since their pay is commission-based. So let's say achieving the goal would allow them to make $300,000 this year. Well, if I just put $300,000 on the table, it's meaningless—it's just paper. It only becomes meaningful when they use it for something. So, I ask, "What will you use that money for?"

Now, some of you reading this book might say, "I don't have salespeople, so how does this apply to me?" Let's say you work with accounting staff. You ask them what their business goal for the year is. Maybe one of their goals is to finish projects three days ahead of the deadline. For example, they prepare a financial report due on the 15th and find it stressful to meet that deadline. Their goal is to get the report done three days earlier. Great. I might think, "I'm not sure how you'll do that," but it doesn't matter what I think.

This is about their ability to create a solution for their own benefit. So I'd ask, "If you were able to finish the report three days early, what would that do for you?" They might say, "Well, I'd be less stressed." Okay, and if you were less stressed, how would that affect your life? They might respond, "I'd be nicer to my family, I'd be nicer to my friends, my blood pressure would go down," and so on.

Whatever the goal is—whether it's money or a feeling—it's what achieving that goal does for them that truly matters. That, my friends, is the real goal. That's what motivates and inspires people to work toward their objectives.

Once I fully understand what they want to achieve, I ask the question that helps me support them: "Would you like me in the boat rowing with you?" Of course, they're going to say "Yes." No one's going to say, "No, I don't want your help." They want you to help.

They want you to participate and to see them succeed. I then tell them, "I am committed to you. I'm in the boat with you. I want you to achieve this. I want this for you."

And now we get to the part you've all been waiting for: how to keep people accountable. The accountability question I pose is, "What should I do, as the caring leader I strive to be, if I see you getting off track?" Now, you can see how accountability is factored in.

I talk to many leaders who complain that they don't know how to keep people accountable. These leaders feel like they need to confront their employees harshly when things go wrong. Of course they feel that way because they've never set up goals with accountability measures agreed upon by the employee. With the conversation I've just outlined, I can now say, if I see them getting off track, "You told me you wanted me in the boat rowing with you, and I'm here. You told me that if I saw you getting off track, you wanted me to help you get back on course. So now I'm stepping up to help you stay on track and achieve your goal."

The other piece of this puzzle related to goal attainment is reward.

Let me give you an example of what that looks like. I had a person, let's call her Shelly, who was a salesperson. Shelly happened to score very high on the influential scale in the DISC system. People with a high "I" tend to lose sight of long-term goals and focus more on immediate gratification. When I asked her what she wanted to achieve, she told me that she really wanted to make a certain amount of money, [X] dollars. I asked her, "Okay, if you're making [X] dollars, what does that do for you?" She explained that she came from a family of nine, with parents who had never left their home in Kansas and had never seen the ocean. She wanted to use some of this money to take her family on a vacation to the beach, where they had never been. She wanted to take her husband, her three children, her eight siblings, and her parents.

Knowing that Shelly needed immediate gratification, I created a reward system for her, as silly as this may sound. Since she wanted to go on a beach vacation, I went to the store and bought small beach-related trinkets—things like gummy fish, a little crystal fish, and a candle that said "beach" on it. You get the idea. I told Shelly that because I was so excited about her goals and what would happen if she achieved them, I wanted to do everything I could to keep her focused on that goal. I told her that every time she made a sale, I would bring her a little gift to keep her on track. Shelly was super excited about that. She loved that kind of stuff. (By the way, I wouldn't enjoy it, as it's not my personality profile.)

She asked, "What if I sell more than one in a week? What happens then?" I said, "No worries, Shelly. I'll give you a gift for every sale you make that week!" Every time Shelly made a sale, I congratulated her and said, "We're one step closer." She was so excited about the gifts. It was like watching a four-year-old at Christmas. It was fun to see.

Shelly started displaying the trinkets on a table in her office. When people came in, they would ask her, "What's that table all about?" She would proudly explain, "My coach is giving me these gifts to help me reach my goal. I'm going to take my whole family on a beach vacation when I hit my sales goal. These are just little reminders that I'm on track."

Now, when Shelly got off track—perhaps going a week or two without a sale or a good prospect—I would step in and say, "Shelly, remember you wanted me to tell you if I saw us getting off track? I see that we're low on prospects. What can we do to increase them?" Maybe we worked on marketing activities or follow-up strategies. Whatever it was, we got things moving again.

What was the end result for Shelly?

I'm thrilled to say that she took her entire family on that beach vacation. The best day in my time as a leader and coach for Shelly was Christmas that year when she gave me a framed picture of her whole family at the beach. The frame said "beach," and she had written on it in gold pen, "I couldn't have done this without you."

Shelly and I were in total alignment. I understood what she wanted, why she wanted it, her personality, and what I needed to do to keep her inspired and engaged. I knew how to hold her accountable and help her achieve the success she wanted and deserved.

Now, that's just one of the many examples of people I've led and coached to success. There's another important piece to goal-setting that I want you to consider. Locke and Latham's goal-setting research shows that when people set goals they believe are easy to achieve, they rarely—let me repeat that, *rarely*—achieve them. It's part of human nature. What their research found is that if you ask someone to set a stretch goal, a goal that pushes them to stretch mentally, educationally, and in their work ethic, they are much more likely to hit or exceed that goal than they are to achieve a simple one.

In our goal-setting conversations, we always focus on the stretch goal, not the easy-to-achieve goal. That's also why the company I worked for saw such a huge increase in sales. We always discussed stretch sales goals, not the easy targets.

Now, some of you may be wondering, what happens if someone doesn't hit their stretch goal? What's the downside? Great question! Even if they don't hit the stretch goal, they'll likely perform better than they would have if they had set an easier goal. Some people ask, "Doesn't that demotivate them?" It could, if you haven't set it up properly. Both you and the employee need to understand that the stretch goal is an aspirational best-case scenario. We're just trying to see how high we can possibly fly with no failure associated with not hitting the goal.

A couple of caveats:

Number one, a stretch goal should *never*—again, *never*—be shared with upper management. Upper management tends to focus only on the stretch goal and ignore the basic goal. When the stretch goal isn't met, they view the employee as a poor performer. Our aim is to create superstars by consistently hitting or exceeding the basic goal!

One of the key things you need to do in this conversation is to make sure people know that the stretch goal we're working toward is between you and them—no one else. You promise them that no one else will know what their stretch goal is. Now, how much more satisfying is it to celebrate when someone hits their stretch goal? For example, if someone hits or exceeds their stretch goal, then I would tell upper-level leaders. I might say, "Karen's basic goal was six sales this month, but her stretch goal was nine, and she hit nine!"

Wow, how cool is that? Everyone gets to applaud Karen, and Karen feels fantastic about it. If Karen doesn't hit the stretch goal, but her basic goal was six, and she hit seven or eight—or even just six—that's still a reason to celebrate. We're still equal to or better than what we expected. Even hitting the basic goal is worth celebrating!

I want to recap here: When you set goals, it's all about the emotional payoff the person perceives they'll get by achieving that goal. The most important thing you can do is understand what that goal is and why it's so critically important to them. Every time you have a conversation and they're off track, the conversation should be, "I'm rowing the boat with you, and it's not okay with me for *you* not to get what you want. I see you working hard, and I want to make sure you achieve what you're striving for. You deserve it."

Isn't this approach a lot more motivational and exciting compared to the usual, "Hey, you're behind plan. The company needs you to hit six sales, so what are we going to do to get to six?" Then your employee responds with, "I could have told you we wouldn't get to six. I don't know why you're harping on that," and they give up.

Some of you reading this book are leaders in sales organizations, and here's my controversial take: You're never working within the Universal Principle of Alignment if you use a leaderboard. A leaderboard creates competition, and someone may have sold you the idea that great salespeople must love to compete. Not true!

If we accept that everyone has different needs and skill sets, it follows that not everyone wants to compete to be number one. In one organization I worked with, one of the founders said to me, "It's a good thing we're not on the sales floor together, or we'd be fighting to be number one."

I responded, "No, you're wrong."

She was taken aback and asked what I meant. She assumed I always wanted to be number one.

I explained, "No, I don't. I'd always be in your top 5%, but I don't need my name next to the number one slot. I have goals I want to achieve that may or may not lead to being number one."

Many of the people we work with are motivated by achievement. They've set their own goals—whether sales goals, personal goals, health goals, or whatever—and if they achieve them, they're ecstatic. It's not about being compared to others.

The purpose of the leaderboard is to make those who aren't on top feel bad about their performance. Psychological research shows that people at the bottom often give up because they feel they can never catch up. People in the middle may try for a while, but when they don't make progress, they start making excuses, saying, "That person got the best territory because they're number one."

Now the excuses start piling up. So if you're using a leaderboard for sales, I'm going to suggest you get rid of it today. You're demotivating more people than you're motivating. You're only motivating the top 5% of your team and demotivating the other 95%.

Why? Because your numbers aren't aligned with their achievement goals. The process I just walked you through ensures alignment with people's individual goals.

Let's also address the idea that rewards shape performance. If you want better performance, give people rewards.

Now, with Shelly's high-I personality (high score on the I profile of the DISC assessment), I gave her lots of small rewards along the way. Consistent reward systems worked great for her. Unfortunately, for many, if you keep giving rewards for every good performance, the reward becomes an expectation. I often get asked whether a financial incentive will improve performance. The answer is yes; it'll work in the short term, but not the long term. I'll cover this more in Chapter 7, on the **Universal Principle of Motivation**.

Now, I know your next question is, "But what if the goals they set are way too low?" That's an easy conversation, too.

A lot of times, people set very low goals or are afraid to set goals because they don't want to be embarrassed. They don't want to fail. You've got to understand that about people. So, when they come up with a subpar goal, the question is always the same: "What are you hopeful that achieving this goal will do for you?" For example, the goal they've given might be the same as what they achieved last year. You can ask, "Is your life any better this year than last year?" And if they say, "No, not really," then you can follow up with, "Well, what can we do to make your life better? How can we adjust these goals to get you a different result?"

Do you see what I'm saying? It's not about telling them their goal is substandard. It's about asking them questions and guiding them to realize that the goal they've set won't help them achieve what they want in life. This way, I've earned the right to work with them to reframe their goal and help them reach what they truly want.

What I'm doing is gaining an understanding of where they want to go by listening to what they tell me. This is how we become strategically aligned. Now, guess what? Our values, strategies, and goals are in alignment because I started with the individuals who need to achieve in order for the company to thrive.

For your action plan, I would ask you to script out what your goal-setting conversation would look like with an employee whom you want to see achieve better results this year. Go through the process I outlined. Choose an employee to start with. Don't pick the most difficult employee. Try it out with someone you already have a good relationship with.

Write the script for what you would say, then practice it. If you don't practice and you flub it, people won't be in alignment with you either. People are afraid of change, and when you come to them with a new approach that you don't seem comfortable with, they may think it's just some new thing you're trying out that doesn't have any real purpose. So, get your script together and practice, practice, practice. Then, find the person you have the best relationship with and work on getting aligned with that individual.

I can assure you that if you adopt this Universal Principle of Alignment, your relationship with your employees and those you lead will be forever changed.

ACTION PLAN

Employee you choose_____

Script_____

_____

_____

_____

_____

_____

_____

_____

_____

_____

_____

_____

_____

_____

_____

_____

_____

_____

_____

_____

THREE

THE UNIVERSAL PRINCIPLE
OF DIVERGENCE

What does divergence mean? When you look at a path you're going down, you can either continue on that path, or you can diverge and take a different approach —a different path.

That's what divergence is truly about—taking a different path. What I'd love for you all to understand right here is that no situation or experience has to remain the same. No situation or experience has to remain the same.

Every one of you and every person you lead has the opportunity to diverge from your current thoughts to different ones. So, what does divergence mean in the professional world? To me, it's about looking at things from a 180-degree different perspective. Divergence is important in our current world because, in business today, problems, challenges, and opportunities constantly arise. What I often see is leaders getting caught in the same whirlpool, going down, down, down, because they view the issue from only one perspective.

They fail to look at the challenge in a different way. What if we approached everything we do with a fresh perspective? That's what I talked about in a previous chapter on the word "perspective." Perspective is how we look at things; it's not the same as perception. Perception is our view of reality, while perspective is about pulling ourselves up, looking at the situation from a 30,000-foot view, and asking, "What am I seeing down there?" Without emotional involvement, without the baggage of hurts and trials, we can look at the situation more objectively and see how perspective and divergence can help us.

Let me tell you a story about how perspective and divergence can change things. Back in the late 1990s, I purchased a home-building company. During the process of purchasing that company from a gentleman we'll call Herbert, someone I had worked with previously, my past came back to haunt me.

I had been married to a lawyer. He was a narcissist and very manipulative. I didn't fully understand how manipulative he was until years later. He was an expert at finding and exploiting my insecurities. Now, I want to make it clear—I'm not blaming him. Nobody can prey on your insecurities unless you allow them to. I went through a difficult emotional time after our divorce, which came after 17 years of marriage. I still felt insecure, like I didn't have everything I needed to be successful.

That previous marriage left me feeling damaged and unworthy, and Herbert was able to tap into that sense of damage and unworthiness. I allowed him to convince me that I should buy the company with a man we'll call Tim, someone who had worked for Herbert for many years. Herbert told me that Tim and I should be partners because Tim was better than me at finance and purchasing. Herbert told me my expertise was in sales and marketing, and that I needed someone to handle the areas where I wasn't as strong. Herbert said Tim could help me. It sounded great at the time, but deep down, I knew it was a bad idea. Yet, I still went along with it.

I can tell you now—it was a bad idea. Tim often wouldn't show up to work, or he would leave immediately when his wife called. She ran the show, and he went home at the worst possible times. Tim never seemed to get anything done. Whenever I asked him for the information I needed, he always said he was "working on it." Everything felt like it was falling on my shoulders. I was at work early, stayed late, and worked weekends. I was miserable.

I was working hard, putting in more hours than necessary, and giving everything I had to make the business successful. But because I went into it with the wrong person, the wrong mindset, and the wrong perspective, I made a bad decision. Facing all these issues, I found myself waking up every day angry.

In the midst of my anger and disappointment, I had a conversation with my stepdad, complaining about my situation for what felt like the millionth time—just like we all do when we get stuck in a loop of complaining about what's bothering us. While I was going on and on, my stepdad told me I should read a book by Arnold M. Patent called *You Can Have It All: A Simple Guide to a Joyful and Abundant Life*. Well, that sounded great to me because I wasn't living an abundant or joyful life. So, I started reading the book, and I was getting excited about life again until I hit a chapter that said, "Whatever you're experiencing now is exactly what you wanted in life." Wow! That was mentally difficult to even begin to absorb.

I got angry just reading that. It said that whatever I'm experiencing now is exactly what I wanted in my life—that I had brought all of this upon myself. I thought, "How could that possibly be? I wanted this business. I brought this guy along because I thought he would help me. I thought I was doing a great job. I really wanted to be successful. I wanted to prove something to the people in my life." (Not a good idea, by the way.) Anyway, I wanted this, but now you're telling me I wanted this nightmare named Tim? You've got to be kidding me. I didn't think so. I got mad and slammed the book down right there. I was done reading. But you know how it is when something resonates, even though you don't want to accept it? It keeps picking at you, over and over, coming back to your mind. I thought about it for a long time.

At that point in time, I had also achieved a lifelong goal: becoming the first woman president of the Dallas Home Builders Association. Imagine how that felt. I owned a home-building company, and these men in my world—whom I had worked so hard to impress, to show I was worthy of being president—might now see me as a failure.

Oh my gosh, it was tearing me up inside. I saw everything as a failure. I felt there was no way out. I felt stuck. It was so bad that I remember having dinner with two of my best friends, and they stopped the dinner to say, "Deb, we're really worried about you. You actually look sick. We're concerned that if you keep stressing like this, you're going to have a heart attack and die." I was 48 years old.

I was so stressed out. I didn't know what to do. I cried a lot. This was now 2006, which created another reason I didn't want to leave the business: It was the height of the home-building boom before the Great Recession in 2008. I felt like I was failing on every level.

We had some ranch property where we would go to spend long weekends. Now, we actually live there. So we decided it was time to go out to the ranch that weekend and let me decompress. That trip was invaluable because, at the ranch, we had no cell service, no internet, no TV—just DVDs. All we had was quiet, nature, my two dogs at the time, and my husband. That weekend, I had the chance to enjoy nature, peace, and quiet. No TV, no radio, nothing. And then, I heard it loud and clear from the universe.

I heard it loud and clear, and it still makes me tear up even today. What I heard was, "This all has to do with how you are looking at things." It was at that point that I figured out how to create a framework that is tied to the **Universal Principle of Divergence**. I'm going to give you an acronym for it to make it easy to remember: **D.A.R.E.**

So, what does D stand for?

You might guess since we're talking about the Universal Principle of Divergence. D stands for taking the exact opposite thought process about your situation. **D is** *divergence*—a 180-degree shift in thinking. In the situation I just told you about, instead of feeling stuck, I decided to take the opposite approach. I wasn't stuck—there were plenty of options. The moment I started believing that I wasn't stuck and that there were multiple options, the Universal Principle of Divergence kicked in. When I began to *diverge* in my thought process, what do you think started happening? Because I now believed and allowed this new perspective to take hold, my fear began to wane. Instead of no options, I had plenty of options.

Now we get to A—**A is for** *action.*

Once I believed my situation was different—that I was no longer stuck and had lots of opportunities—I started investigating what those opportunities were. I wrote down all the possible options, and I was so happy. I was happy because I was able to take advantage of all the possibilities I had. One of those options was closing the business, an option I would never have considered before, and the option I ultimately chose because I was so unhappy.

What I really realized was that I was unhappy not just because of the events or the wrong choices I had made but because this was not my calling. My calling wasn't to run a home-building company to prove to all the guys or my dad that I could do it. My calling was to teach, and in this job, I no longer taught. I no longer developed people or helped them grow. That's another reason I was so unhappy: because if I had truly had a passion for running the business, I would have figured out how to deal with Tim. But I was miserable because I was doing something every day that wasn't my calling, wasn't my passion, and wasn't what I was meant to do. My unhappiness became unbearable.

Now we get to the next letter, R. **R is for** *results.*

When you take a divergent thought as the new path, it leads to determining what action you want to take. That action gives you the result. What I learned is that if you see a situation differently, you are likely going to act differently. And if you act differently, you cannot possibly get the same result!

In this situation, I went down the diverging path. Instead of believing I was stuck with no options, I decided I *did* have options. When I thought I was stuck, the actions I took were to suffer and work myself into the ground. I acted as if I had to live with my situation. But once I realized I wasn't stuck, that was the shift in action I took.

With this new perspective—that I had options—I was able to write down all the potential solutions. I asked myself, "Why do I feel this way? Is it really just about Tim, or is there something else going on?" When I took action to reflect on this and explore my emotions, I realized I was unhappy for many reasons. I realized the best course of action was to shut the business down.

The result? That day became one of the happiest days I can remember during the 10 years I owned that business! I was no longer stuck! I was free to have a fulfilling life and find something more aligned with my passions and interests. And while some of my homebuilder friends made comments about "quitting the business" during one of the best years in home building at the time, they sang a different tune in 2009. Suddenly, they were applauding me for my decision. They thought I was the smart one!

The last letter is **E, which stands for *emotion*.**

I shut the business down—the happiest day of my life. Now, here's the E: *emotion*. Each situation we experience evokes an emotion. Negative emotions push us away from taking that action again, while positive emotions encourage us to replicate that action. That's how adults learn, right? So, the emotion tied to an experience is equally important. As your perspective changes or as divergence occurs, an action is taken, which gives you a result. And when you take a different action, you can't possibly get the same result, which fosters a different emotion.

When we learn to take different actions to gain different results, we evoke different emotions. That's just how it works. So, with the Universal Principle of Divergence, understanding that you can align with the universe and that it's offering you different ways and options, you embrace that and take different actions. You'll get a different result and a different emotion.

Let's take a leader I work with, whom we'll call "George." George was very frustrated because he had an employee he really disliked. This employee seemed to derail everything—George's department, production, results, and more—at every turn.

I asked George, "Why do you think this guy doesn't like you?" George started listing the employee's transgressions: not showing up to work on time, speaking disrespectfully, and not keeping promises. I then asked, "Do you think there could be other reasons for his behavior besides disliking you?"

George thought for a while and said, "Actually, there might be."

I asked what those reasons could be.

He said, "Well, we were super busy when we hired him. He got some training, but not everything he needed. I think some of the tasks I'm giving him are things he doesn't really know how to do well, and he doesn't want to ask for my help."

I said, "Okay, George, let's go with that. Let's change your perspective and diverge from the idea that this guy doesn't like you. Instead, let's explore the idea that maybe he needs training." George adopted this mindset, and I asked him what action he would take.

He said, "I'm going to sit down with him, talk about what he knows, what he doesn't know, where he feels confident, and where he's struggling. I'll also ask his coworkers where they think he excels and where he's falling short. Then we'll come up with an action plan."

After George had that conversation, the employee admitted, "Yes, I don't show up on time, and maybe I'm a little disrespectful. But I don't feel respected because I didn't get the training I needed.

I've been asking for more training, but I haven't received it, and I feel left behind. So, why wouldn't I act this way?"

George responded, "What if we get you the training you need? What if I give you the support you're asking for? Would that help?" The employee agreed that it would.

Guess what happened? They gave him the training he needed. He started showing up to work on time, stopped being disrespectful, and developed a fantastic relationship with George that continues to this day.

The emotional result for George was, "You know what? I've helped this person. It was really on me. I'm the one who created this situation for him, not the other way around. I took a divergent path and chose to believe that this guy needed my help. I asked if he needed my help, we got him the support he needed, and everything began to change. I feel so good and empowered by this."

That's how powerful the Universal Principle of Divergence is. We get so caught up in seeing things one way, believing someone else is conspiring against us, when, in fact, it's us not realizing that our choices brought us to this point. And as Arnold M. Patent's book taught me, it was true.

I had my issues with Tim because I made all the choices that led me there. It wasn't Tim's fault. I should have never brought him on as a partner. That was my fault. No one forced me to take Tim on.

And yet, my concerns about what others thought of me were also consuming my thoughts and clouding my perspective. My friends asked me, "Are the people you're worried about going to take care of you if you have a heart attack or get sick? No. So does it really matter what they think about you? Doesn't it really matter what you think about yourself?" I will never forget that conversation. Thank God I had two women who loved me enough as friends to say what needed to be said.

Unfortunately, my poor husband (my second husband) just kept trying to comfort me and support me in any decision I wanted to make. But that wasn't making me happy—it was only making me angrier because I was looking for someone else to create the path for me. The universe made me realize that I needed to choose that divergent path myself. I did, and I chose to diverge from the path I was on.

I then took different actions and got different results. Emotionally, I was relieved, and I began to head down a path that led me to where I am today. It led me to take on the role of director of training for a multi-billion-dollar company. It led me to create my own consulting and coaching practice. I've got to tell you, I'm the happiest I've ever been. I am fulfilled. I love my life.

So here's what I want you to do for your action plan related to this chapter: Take an event in your life right now—anything you think is negative—and create a vision of the exact opposite.

For example, if you think someone doesn't like you because they said something rude, try taking the divergent path like George did. Instead of thinking, *They don't like me,* think, *Maybe they're afraid.* Why would they be afraid? Line out the options you have. What opportunities do you have? What's the exact opposite of the way you're seeing the situation?

Now, what actions will you take? Go and take those actions. Then, write down the results you got and the emotions you felt. This way, it becomes part of how you approach every opportunity and challenge in your life. I can assure you with every fiber of my being that if you adopt this Universal Principle of Divergence, whenever you face any opportunity in life, you will come out a different and forever changed person in a way that is so positive and miraculous, you'll wonder why you never did this before.

ACTION PLAN

The Challenge

_____

D

_____
_____
_____
_____
_____

A

_____
_____
_____
_____
_____

R

_____
_____
_____
_____
_____

E

_____
_____
_____
_____
_____

FOUR
THE UNIVERSAL PRINCIPLE OF CHOICE

What is the **Universal Principle of Choice**? Common sense suggests that every event in our lives is shaped by the choices we make, consciously or subconsciously. Just think about that. Based on all the conversations I've had with people I've worked with, and even in my own life, I've found that many of the choices that shape our lives are made subconsciously. In fact, if you read the experts, they will tell you that 95% of what you do every day is controlled by your subconscious mind, not your conscious mind.[1] If your conscious mind is only engaged about 5% of the time, that should concern all of us. How many things have we learned or have been told that now reside in our subconscious mind, affecting every choice we make? It's pretty astounding.

Now, what is the actual definition of choice as we're discussing it here? It involves looking at all the possibilities available to us, evaluating those possibilities, and then coming to a decision about

---

1. Lipton, Bruce. *The Biology of Belief: Unleashing the Power of Consciousness, Matter & Miracles*. Carlsbad, CA: Hay House, Inc, 2016.

what action to take. Choices are not only based on what we are consciously aware of while evaluating these possibilities but also on what our subconscious is doing to weigh in on the options. I think that's an important thing to remember.

So, let's talk about choices in the context of leading people. How people present themselves to us is always interesting. Many times, an employee might act one way in a situation and then act differently in a seemingly identical situation. Have you ever had that happen? Many of my leaders are confused by this. An analogy that might help explain this involves the emotional triggers people carry, which can affect their choices. Imagine walking through an airport. You see people lugging their carry-on bags packed full of things. You don't know what's in those bags, but to the person carrying them, the contents are important enough to keep close.

This is similar to the emotional triggers leaders encounter when working with people. Leaders need to understand how these triggers affect decision-making. That emotional "bag" is packed full, and we don't always know what's in it. We don't need to fully unpack it, but we need to understand that it's there.

When you find yourself in a challenging situation, remember that according to the Universal Principle of Choice, every experience we go through is shaped by the choices we make. Therefore, any opportunity we face requires us to accept full responsibility for the situation.

If you don't have the right employees, why did you choose to hire them? I understand that sometimes we make choices because we feel forced to. What do I mean by that? Let's use the example of hiring. Suppose someone quits suddenly, and you don't have anyone else to fill the position. You rush to fill the vacancy and end up hiring whoever you can find. However, I would argue that your choice not to continue recruiting, networking, and engaging with potential candidates regularly is why you find yourself in a position where you have to hire "a body" instead of the right person.

That choice puts you in a position where you're forced to take what's available because you didn't plan for possible situations. As I mentioned in another chapter, the choice I made to take on a business partner who wasn't the right fit affected me in so many ways. It impacted me emotionally, physically, and mentally, leaving me at a loss for how to deal with my life—until I realized, based on what I read in *You Can Have It All*, that I needed to take responsibility for the choices I made.

When discussing the Universal Principle of Choice, especially in leadership, we need to understand that self-awareness of our choices is critical. Think about the fact that your subconscious mind operates 95% of the time. How many choices are you making consciously? What subconscious actions are leading you down a path to an experience you may or may not want?

Living in the present moment and becoming self-aware of your choices every time you make one is crucial. There are also two biases I want to address in relation to choices: overconfidence bias and confirmation bias. Overconfidence bias, according to research, means that we overestimate our ability to make the right decision. Confirmation bias means we favor information that supports our preexisting beliefs. When we're making choices or decisions, we tend to align with information that confirms beliefs we already hold. I see this most often in leaders during the hiring process.

When I talk to most leaders, they often tell me they go into an interview, talk to the candidate for a while, and trust their gut instinct about who to hire. However, psychological research[2] shows that hiring based on gut instinct can lead to more bad hires than good ones. Why? Because of confirmation bias, which is the tendency to seek out information that supports what we already believe.

Let's take this example: I'm going to hire someone to work at my company, and I go out to meet them in the reception lobby. For

---

2. Woods, Tyler. "Why Intuition May Lead Employers Astray When Hiring." *Psychology Today*, May 23, 2023.

this example, let's presume that before I arrived, the receptionist gave them something cold to drink. It's a hot day, and the Coke can is sweaty and cold. The applicant sees me coming and hands the Coke can to the receptionist so they're ready to shake my hand. We say hello; I reach out, shake their hand, and think, *Oh gosh, cold, clammy, wet—ick.* Now, I've made a judgment. I have a bias, right? I think this person with a cold, clammy, wet hand isn't confident and seems anxious. At this point, my overconfidence bias and confirmation bias take over. So, when we sit down for the interview, what happens? I throw hardball questions at them—questions that are difficult to answer.

Why?

Because I have to support my belief that this person isn't a good hire for me.

Now, let's take the exact opposite scenario. I go out and shake someone's hand, and they have a firm handshake. They're dressed nicely, they have a great smile, and immediately I think, *Wow, this is a great person.* Remember, we make a judgment call on someone within the first tenth of a second of meeting them. You read that right! Princeton psychologists Willis and Todorov did a study[3] showing that within one-tenth of a second, we form an impression of someone, and longer exposure doesn't change that initial impression! So now, when I take this person back for the interview, what do you think I do? My confirmation bias tells me, "Hey, this is a great person."

To support my belief that this person is great, I start asking softball questions—easy ones that allow them to sail through the interview. I create a smooth, pleasant conversation. At the end of the day, when I'm done interviewing, guess what? I believe they're a great hire.

---

3. Wargo, E. "How Many Seconds to a First Impression?" Association for Psychological Science - APS, July 1, 2006. https://www.psychologicalscience.org/observer/how-many-seconds-to-a-first-impression.

But are they really?

This is where our gut instinct, influenced by overconfidence bias—where we overestimate our ability to make the right decision —can lead us astray in our choices. So, how do you avoid this as a leader? How do we avoid making the wrong choice? How do we become aware of this Universal Principle of Choice and use it to our benefit? We have to remember that the choices we make shape our future. They shape the events to come. They determine future consequences, both positive and negative.

How can we do a better job of avoiding negative consequences? By adopting the use of a structured interview. Studies show that structured interviews result in better hiring decisions than unstructured ones, which we described in the example above. In a structured interview, the process is applied consistently to all applicants.

You should have a set of interview questions that you ask every person you interview. The idea that you adjust your questions based on how the interview is going is what creates overconfidence bias. It allows you to believe you're making a great gut decision. Then, when you make a decision based on your confirmation bias, you alter the scope of the interview and change the questions. However, when you use an interview process that treats all applicants the same, with the same set of questions, instead of changing it based on how you feel about the interview, don't you think you might get a different outcome? Can you begin to see how the choice to implement a structured approach might lead to better results than relying on your impressions?

If you're being logical, you have to say yes to that.

There's another piece to this puzzle that will make you a better interviewer: creating a score sheet. Let's use this example. In the real estate world, when working with people in home sales for a builder, we created a score sheet based on what we needed people to do in their job. Here's an example: One of the key responsibilities for these employees was self-marketing, not just relying on the company's marketing to drive prospects to them. One of our structured questions was, "How have you generated prospects for a neighborhood you were working in when there wasn't a lot of foot traffic?" On the score sheet we created, we had a category for *Prospecting*. If, for example, they said, "Oh, I reached out to all of my realtor contacts and used them to bring me prospective buyers," they'd score a two on a scale of six.

Now, if they also added, "Not only did I work with realtors, I also tapped into my referral base. I called previous home buyers, people I knew in the industry, and asked for referrals," they'd score another two points, bringing their total to four.

And then, if they said, for example, that they used social media to help drive traffic by posting every week, or maybe they went out and partnered with local businesses to create a marketing strategy that drove prospects to their neighborhood, they might score six points. They'd get six out of six. So, when we went through this process, we were able to objectively score candidates based on their capabilities, not subjectively based on our impressions of them. By choosing to set up a process that allows me to objectively evaluate potential recruits, I'm making a choice that is more likely to lead to a positive result.

Now, let's add another layer to help overcome the biases I might have. That additional layer would be to have multiple people interview the candidate. Once those interviews are completed, we can have a panel discussion to share our thoughts about the applicant.

Many employers today opt for panel interviews, where multiple people ask questions simultaneously. Personally, I don't buy into that. I understand the reasoning behind it and see potential positives, such as putting people under pressure. But I have to ask, do all the people you hire face that kind of pressure regularly? What about the personalities that fold under pressure and scrutiny? What about those who can't take tests well but know the subject matter inside and out? Are you filtering out those kinds of people?

I believe that having a panel discussion about an applicant is far more effective. What we did with one of our clients was to create an interview structure where four or five different people interviewed the applicant at different times. Then, all the interviewers got together to review their scores and discuss how their interviews went. Since all the interviewers used the same structured interview process, with structured questions and score sheets, the panel was instrumental in helping the company make the best decision.

Another area where we face the Universal Principle of Choice is in getting people to choose our direction. How do we get someone to choose to follow us?

One way is through how we respond and talk to people. If we frame team members' decisions as creating a potential loss for us, we create a workforce that behaves in a risk-averse manner. In some cases, that might be beneficial, but in other cases, it's not—especially in rapidly changing markets, which we all face at one time or another. Why wouldn't we want people to adopt behaviors that involve some risk, particularly if they're well-considered?

Conversely, I can help people choose a different path by framing their choices as creating potential gains for us. Now, my friends, we're encouraging them to take risks.

With the Universal Principle of Choice, we've discussed how my choices affect my team, as seen in the hiring example, and how I can apply the principle to help shape the choices made by those I lead. When people believe their choices create potential loss, they become risk-averse. When you frame their choices as creating potential gains for themselves or the company, they are more likely to take risks, which can be beneficial.

Now, let's explore another aspect of choice: Choices are also based on our ability to think critically. So, what is critical thinking? Critical thinking is about assessing and evaluating situations so that you can make a judgment about how to proceed. When we face a problem, critical thinking allows us to break it down, examine all its parts, and come up with a solution—that is a choice.

If you've had any higher education—college-level education, for example—you're fortunate because much of higher education enhances our critical thinking skills. We are asked to analyze different subject matter, think about the consequences of applying knowledge to various situations, and consider different perspectives. People who integrate knowledge from various fields also tend to have more well-developed critical thinking skills. If you've worked in different industries and can draw from what you've learned and apply it across fields, that also fosters critical thinking.

Interestingly, digital media has limited our ability to think critically. What happens when people consume or gather misinformation from social media? They may bring that misinformation into the workplace and use it in their decision-making process, potentially leading to poor choices.

Also, many of our workers, who spend a lot of time on digital media, have shorter attention spans. This impairs their ability to think deeply and reflectively about subjects that require the critical analysis necessary for effective decision-making.

Why am I always talking about analysis and decision-making? Because both are directly related to choice. The challenge with today's digital media society is that it has created echo chambers, where our existing beliefs and confirmation biases are reinforced by the information we consume. In these environments, there is little exposure to diverse perspectives, and our beliefs are rarely challenged.

Our beliefs and confirmation biases also affect planning as leaders. If we don't brainstorm, if we don't involve all members of our leadership team, if we don't allow people to make their own choices—which creates accountability—we won't have a solid plan. And without a strategy, a plan, or accountability, how can you possibly determine your success or your future?

I hope you can see the impact your choices have and the critical role they play in your success as a leader. The choices you've made up to this point are the ones that got you here.

Sometimes, the "here" we arrive at is great. Other times, as I've described in my own life, it's not so great. But we must become very self-aware about our choices so we can move toward different outcomes, connecting with *all* of the other options in our universe and all the possibilities to choose from. This allows us to get the result we *want* and not the one we don't!

As a leader, you also need to think about how to help those you lead make better choices. How do you help them understand the potential gain they can achieve by making great decisions? How do you help them grasp the importance of critical thinking in shaping their choices? How do you guide them in seeing the solutions available to them? You can only do this if you teach the concept of choice and the Universal Principle of Choice.

Hopefully, you can now see that when we teach people how to analyze arguments, assess evidence, and reason through their judgments—and when we help them understand that every event is shaped by the choices they make—we empower those we lead. When we fully understand, accept, and become self-aware of the choices we make, how different could life be?

Your action plan for this chapter is to reflect on two or three experiences you've had (whether in the distant past or more recent) and assess all the choices you made leading up to those events that brought you to where you are today. I also suggest that you look not only at negative outcomes but at positive ones as well. Too often, we focus only on negative experiences to improve ourselves when, in fact, we should also examine positive experiences to understand what we did right so we can replicate more of those successes.

I hope this chapter has helped you understand that our choices are shaped by our biases, values, and emotional triggers and that making great choices is about being self-aware. Our choices can make or break us as leaders, and we must also recognize that the choices our employees make can do the same for us. By understanding this, we can truly succeed.

ACTION PLAN

Experience One: Choices and Results

_____
_____
_____
_____
_____
_____
_____

Experience Two: Choices and Results

_____
_____
_____
_____
_____
_____
_____

Experience Three: Choices and Results

_____
_____
_____
_____
_____
_____
_____

FIVE

THE UNIVERSAL PRINCIPLE
OF FOCUS

L et's first look at the definition of *focus*. The definitions typically say that focus is our main purpose or interest. Now, let's define the **Universal Principle of Focus**. What we focus on tends to expand in our lives. Take a moment to really think about what that means. I'll repeat it again: What we focus on tends to expand in our lives.

I don't know if any of you have read books by Dr. Joe Dispenza, who is one of my favorite authors. I've listened to his podcasts, and I've seen him speak in person. If you don't know about him, he is deeply involved in the neuroscience of our brains—why we do the things we do, why we believe what we believe, and how we can change those beliefs.

His personal story is quite miraculous. He was in a biking accident during a triathlon, where he was thrown from his bike after being hit by a car, breaking his back in multiple places. At the time, he was a chiropractor, and four different orthopedic surgeons told him he would need surgery that would alleviate his pain but leave him paralyzed for life.

Dispenza chose not to have the surgery. Instead, he decided to focus on healing himself. And within eight weeks, he had done just that. In about 12 weeks, he was back competing in triathlons. Why do I bring up someone like Dr. Dispenza?

I think his experience clearly shows how valuable and important your focus is. To heal himself, he focused on visualizing a healed spine, which he could do well, given his background as a chiropractor.

Now, he admitted it took him a good six weeks to stop thinking about all the negative things, like whether he should sell his practice, wondering if he would ever walk again—all the negative thoughts that arise for all of us. But he kept shifting his focus to visualize the healing of his broken vertebrae and his physical recovery.

Now, let's look at you as a leader and discuss where your focus tends to expand in your leadership life. What does that look like? Let's talk about your focus.

First, let's talk about the many leaders who believe they can multitask. I hear it all the time: "I'm a great multitasker." Well, research says you're wrong about that. The ability to multitask is a myth.[1]

In reality, when you take your focus off the task at hand, you actually work at a slower pace. This is tied to a common complaint I frequently hear from leaders: "I can't get everything done. I have a time management problem." What I tell those I coach and develop is, "I don't think you have a time management problem—I think you have a focus problem."

When I begin working with many of these leaders, I describe their day, and they often tell me how frequently they are interrupted. They lose focus on the task at hand and focus only on the immediate "emergency" in front of them. Sometimes, of course,

---

1. Choate, Laura. "The Myth of Multitasking: Why Research Shows It's Not Productive for Parents or Teens." *Psychology Today*, May 20, 2016.

true emergencies arise, but not everything people bring to you is an emergency.

These leaders don't have a clear plan for how they will handle their day. They allow others to set their priorities. So this multitasking they believe they're so good at actually increases their mental load. If you're multitasking a lot, that's part of the reason you feel so tired at the end of the day. Jumping from one activity to another actually increases the mental demand on you—and certainly decreases your productivity!

Multitasking also reduces your ability to rely on automatic behaviors. One thing you learn in psychology is that your subconscious mind looks for patterns. It's the biggest "hacker" ever. Your conscious mind can't handle all the distractions it faces in the world, so your subconscious mind steps in to process things automatically.

You might think, *Oh, Deb, that can't be true.* But it is, and I'll give you an example everyone can relate to. If you frequently drive to any place, how many times have you driven home from work, to the store, or somewhere else you go often—and when you get to your destination, you realize you don't even remember how you got there? You left point A, and suddenly, you're at point B. You finish your trip and think, *Oh my gosh, I don't even remember how I got here.*

That's your subconscious at work.

While you're driving, the moment your subconscious recognizes a pattern as to where you are going, it says, "Oh, I know where we're headed. Conscious mind, go ahead and focus on the song you're listening to on the radio." It allows your conscious mind to think about what you're going to have for dinner, what you want to wear, or maybe even remind you to call your mom. Any of those thoughts occupy your conscious mind while your subconscious handles the task of driving. Now, that should scare you a little. So, how do we not end up in accidents more frequently?

Because as soon as the subconscious mind recognizes unfamiliar territory or something it doesn't know how to handle, it brings the conscious mind back into the loop. Let's go back to the driving example: suppose, all of a sudden, brake lights appear in front of you. Suddenly, you snap out of your autopilot mode and hit the brakes. That's your subconscious mind alerting you to a problem ahead and handing control back to your conscious mind. When you think about it, you realize how much stress your subconscious mind takes off your conscious mind by handling tasks that can be done automatically.

When you multitask, however, you decrease your ability to rely on automatic behaviors. By constantly shifting between tasks, you're not allowing your subconscious to take over the routine tasks that make you more productive.

Believe me, I'm not perfect at this either. For example, when I start multitasking—writing a post, switching off to answer an email while I still have the post going—then I finish the email and go back to the post. I look at what I've just written and think, *Oh my gosh, that's grammatically incorrect!* Or, *Wow, I spelled that word wrong. I'm glad I didn't post that, or I'd look like an idiot.*

How many mistakes are you making because you've lost your focus? How many errors happen because you're multitasking?

Multitasking also impairs your cognitive ability. Cognitive ability refers to your ability to think critically. When you keep shifting from task to task, you're not becoming a better critical thinker—you're becoming worse because your brain doesn't have the time to critically analyze and explore solutions. You become far more impulsive. You know those days when you get irritated and blurt something out to an employee because they've frustrated you? Perhaps you should examine how much multitasking you've been doing that day. How much less focused were you, and why did impatience or anger arise? It likely happened because your impulses took over. You were cognitively impaired, working slower, and mentally drained.

Now, if you're anything like me—and I'll admit, I get bored pretty easily—it's important to recognize this. I don't have ADD or ADHD; I just get bored. I love solving problems and taking on challenges. That might be you as well. But switching from task to task, even though it feels like you're breaking up the day, doesn't actually make you more productive. Your focus is scattered. So what should you do instead? Try making a schedule and breaking up tasks into 20-minute intervals. By breaking up your tasks, you can truly focus on them. When your brain starts to wander, as mine does, you can remind yourself that you only have ten more minutes left and refocus.

Here's another little trick: When working on projects as a leader and needing to maintain focus, tackle the painstaking or task-oriented work in the morning. Why? Because your brain is fresher. In the afternoon, focus on more creative tasks. By then, your brain has loosened up. You've already cleared the habitual tasks off your plate, and now you can focus on creation.

Another very effective way to maintain focus is through mindfulness. What is mindfulness? Well, it is somewhat related to meditation, but true mindfulness is about focusing on the present.[2] So many problems in our lives arise because we're thinking about the past or worrying about the future. Think about your life. Think about the situations you find yourself in. Think about your drive home and what occupies your thoughts.

Your focus tends to either be on trying not to repeat the past—reflecting on all the things that have happened, good or bad—or it shifts to worrying about the future and what could happen.

But if you practice mindfulness, you're fully in the present. You're focused on the *now*, engaged with what's happening at the

2. "The Science of Mindfulness: The Ultimate Guide to the Research on the Effects of Mindfulness and Meditation on Our Health, Psyche, and Overall Quality of Life." *Mindful*, August 31, 2022.

moment. The more focused you are on the present, the better the decisions and choices you can make.

You can create so many more options for yourself. You can have more alignment in your life if you focus on the present. I'm sure you've heard this statement before: *The present is a gift*, meaning the present moment is your gift.

I say this to so many people who focus on the past or the future: Face it, you can't go back and change the past. And guess what about the future? You'll never actually *see* it because you're always in the now. You never reach the future. So, wasting your focus, energy, and mental currency on the past or the future keeps you from being the creative genius that we all truly are.

One way you can change your focus and what you focus on throughout the day is by how you start your day. What does that mean? What I suggest to people to improve their focus at work is this: Before you leave work for the day, determine the six most important things you MUST get done the next day. Why six? I'm not exactly sure why it's such a magical number, but I know it works. Let's say today is Tuesday. Before you leave work on Monday, line out the six most important things you commit to doing the next day. Notice I said you have to *commit* to getting those things done before you leave work. You might be thinking this won't work for you or that it's too simple to be effective. But I can tell you, I've taught this to many of my clients, and they've told me what a difference it makes in their focus and productivity.

They say, "I feel like I go home having accomplished more." Well, you do! Many of you have a never-ending to-do list—one that keeps growing but rarely has anything checked off. I know what that feels like. You all feel like you're more important or have more to do, like the world can't function without you because your to-do list is endless. But an endless to-do list is *debilitating*.

I'll repeat that: It is *debilitating*!

People with never-ending to-do lists are the ones who go home feeling like they've accomplished nothing. How could you focus on anything?

So if we change our focus, as the Universal Principle of Focus says—what you focus on grows—can you see how this change will alter your results? If you want to be better at time management, as I said before, become better at managing your focus.

When you leave work each day, you'll have outlined the six most important things you need to do the next day. When you walk into work, your focus will immediately be on what you have *committed* to completing that day. See where the focus is? It's not about opening up your computer to check emails and determine what fire to put out. It's not about listening to all your voicemails to decide whether there's another crisis to handle. It's not about scrolling through social media in the morning. The focus, when you start work each day, should be on the six most important things you need to do. This will change your life immeasurably. Let me give you an example of someone I worked with. Her name is Terry, and she came to me with the same problem: "Deb, I just can't seem to manage my time. I can't seem to get things done. I don't have focus."

The first thing I told Terry to do was create a list of the six most important things. Let me tell you, that was the hardest task Terry had ever done because she had a to-do list of 40 or 50 items.

As we went through the list, she told me all these things were important. I said, "Of course, they're all important. But which six are the *most* important things you must get done before you leave work tomorrow?"

Once she started going through the list, she realized not everything on that list needed to be completed the next day. Once she established that, she walked into the office the next day with focus and a plan. She told me, "Deb, I felt like I had a sense of purpose. I felt like I had a path. I knew where I was going."

The second thing we taught her was how to time-block. You may have heard of this before. I do it a little differently than most. I block out a percentage of time. Now, as I said before, if you like variety in your day, use the 20-minute rule and make your time blocks 20 minutes. Or, if you have a big project, block the time by an hour. Maybe a project will take you multiple days. Then, I might break that big task down into an hour every day for five, six, or seven days.

See, many times when we have a project in front of us, especially one we don't like, we tend to push it off. I am just the same, and so was Terry. We procrastinate, and then what happens? We end up pulling an all-nighter to get it done, and then complain about how difficult the task was. Well, of course, we made it more difficult. Had we broken that task into 20-minute segments and focused on those 20 minutes, or broken it up into an hour every day for seven, eight, or 14 days—whatever the time requirement was— can you see how much easier it would have been to complete the task we didn't really care for? How we might have stopped procrastinating? And think about how much better the work product might have been—how much more mistake-free it could have been. How much more energy would we have had when we left to go home at night?

All of that changes.

So what Terry did was block out her time. Another thing she did was to block out "do not disturb" periods, and she told everyone she worked with that she would respond to emails, texts, and phone calls during certain times. You might be thinking that wouldn't work for you.

Have you tried it? Most people haven't. What I can tell you is that when you let the people you work with know you're working on projects that require your full attention and focus, and that you need to limit the times during which you can take calls, answer texts, or emails, most people will comply. Most people understand. The reason they keep bothering you and knocking on your door now is that they're never sure when you'll get back to them. I can also tell you that when you're multitasking, you don't usually follow up very well. That's why you've increased the problem of people needing immediate attention from you.

The last thing I want to talk about regarding focus is focusing on the person in front of you. I was working with Andrew, a sales manager, a couple of weeks ago. One of his team members had made a comment to me that it was difficult to work with Andrew because they never felt heard. I asked why they felt that way, and they replied, "Well, when I'm talking to Andrew, he's sitting at his desk, looking at things on his phone and then at his computer. And, of course, Andrew has one of those Apple watches, and he's checking what texts or emails are coming in." No wonder this person never felt heard.

Does this apply to you?

People often develop bad behaviors to get noticed when they feel unheard. So maybe some of the dysfunction you experience with team members, or the needy team members who are always asking you 8,000 questions, occurs because you never give them your full focus when they're in front of you. How different would your life be if you eliminated those constant questions? Maybe you'd be reducing the needy behavior.

So, based on this chapter, what I would like you to do as your action plan is to look at your ability to focus.

An easy way to do this is to break your day into hour-long segments. Get a journal, set a timer on your phone for one hour, and at the end of that hour, write down everything you did.

Then do it for another hour. And another hour.

Do this for five consecutive days. I know it's painful to think about, but if you want to change your behavior, the best way is to understand or focus on where you're struggling right now. Once you start to see the pattern of where your focus is going in five days, you'll be able to create a plan to change your focus levels.

As I mentioned at the start of this chapter, what we focus on tends to expand in our lives. And what I really want to leave you with is not just time management tips, the myth of multitasking, or strategies to get things done—but a question about the quality of your life.

Your focus is directly related to the outcomes you are getting in your life. If you are getting negative outcomes, you are most likely focusing on negative thoughts. You can change this immediately by putting your focus on the things you DO want. My clients have found that just by making this shift, the outcomes in their lives have changed dramatically for the better!

ACTION PLAN

What I learned from journaling about my time over the last 5 days

---

SIX

THE UNIVERSAL PRINCIPLE
OF EMPOWERMENT

What is empowerment? I think it's a term that's used very loosely, and there's often a misperception about its meaning, especially in a business context. Put simply, empowerment is the process of becoming stronger and more confident.

Some common dictionary definitions suggest that empowerment is the authority or power given to you to control your life and claim your rights. So, how does that apply to the Universal Principle of Empowerment? This principle states that we have the ability to take control of our lives and make decisions that affect us.

Note what those definitions and principles tell us: It's about becoming stronger and more confident, about controlling one's life and claiming one's rights. Let's think about that for a minute—empowerment is the process of becoming stronger and more confident, right?

How do we actually become more empowered? I would say it's by knowing and working on the things that *are* within our power to control and by stopping the effort to control the things that are *not* in our power. This is one of the first things I work on with leaders as it relates to control. We've said that empowerment is the process of people taking control of their own lives and making decisions that affect them, right? That's the **Universal Principle of Empowerment**.

Most leaders who struggle with empowerment are trying to control things they cannot control. For example, I can't control what the economy is going to do tomorrow, can I? No. And yet, if I want to feel empowered to make choices and control my life, and all I do is focus on external factors like the economy, I'll never feel in control or empowered. Why? Because the economy is something I can't control. If you want to feel more empowered as a leader or in your personal life, focus on what you can control, and make decisions about those specific things. When you stick to that principle, you'll find yourself in a much better place.

Empowerment also affects emotions—or maybe it's more accurate to say that a lack of empowerment adversely affects emotions. So many times, people I work with will tell me, "Oh my gosh, Joe made me so mad today by what he said." The first thing I'll ask them is, "Why did you give Joe so much control over your life?" This relates back to the previous chapter on the **Universal Principle of Choice**. Whatever emotion you feel is a choice—you choose to feel it. No one can force you to feel a certain way. So, if you want to feel empowered, think about the choice you are about to make in response to what Joe did or said. Do you want to give him control and power over your life, or would you prefer to keep that power for yourself?

Let's take the example of the economy again. If the economy isn't doing well, do I look at my life negatively because I can't control it, and therefore, conclude that I can't control anything in my life? Do I believe everything is affected by what someone else is doing? I could take that approach—and many people, dysfunctional leaders included, do. But really great leaders and the truly successful people in this world take a different approach. They say,

"I can't control what's out there, but I can control what I do every day to get the results I want."

Think about it. If you look back at pictures from the Great Depression—because most people reading this book didn't experience it firsthand—you'll see many images of people standing in soup lines, waiting to be fed. Yet, I can show you instance after instance of people who never stood in line for food, who had a place to live, and who were relatively unaffected by the economy. My two parents grew up during that time. Neither was homeless, nor did they go without food or clothing. They didn't live in a wealthy neighborhood, and my grandfathers didn't have high-paying jobs, but they made it through.

In fact, my mother's father lost their house during the Great Depression. She remembers having to move from there, but they didn't end up in the soup lines. They rented a home instead. My grandfather even started his own trucking company. He bought a truck and hauled dirt to construction sites. He made it work! I think that's where I get my entrepreneurial spirit from—he saw a need, and he filled it. He believed he could make money, even after losing their home, and he did. That's truly an empowered individual. He didn't succumb to the negative thinking of the times or believe that his family's future would be entirely dictated by the economy. He controlled what he could: his actions, beliefs, and thoughts.

So, the empowered choice leads us to ask ourselves *What can I control?* And those things I can control are what I should focus on in my life. See how these ideas all connect? The choices, the focus—all of these universal principles. The belief that everything I want is within reach. These are the things that lead to an empowered life.

There's a book you might want to read called *Power vs. Force* by David R. Hawkins, M.D., Ph.D. The book deals with levels of consciousness. Higher levels of consciousness relate to concepts like love, altruism, and dedication to principles, while lower levels of consciousness are associated with survival and self-interest. Think about that for a moment. How many of you have worked with leaders who embodied either of these qualities? I know I've worked with both. The leaders who led from a place of survival and self-interest were rarely successful, and more importantly, they were not well-liked or respected by those they led. It was quite the opposite with leaders who led from a place of altruism and principle.

Hawkins' concepts are incredibly significant when it comes to discussing empowerment. He explains that leaders lower on the scales of consciousness lead from a place of force, while those higher on the scale lead from a place of power. What's the difference? Many leaders believe that force *is* power and that when you have the ability to make people do something—using force—you are the empowered individual. However, Hawkins makes it very clear that this kind of thinking is wrong. He suggests that power is *never* about force; it's about living in such a way that people are drawn to you. Leaders using force are seen as insecure and self-centered, while those who are dedicated to principles and altruism are seen as confident, and people naturally gravitate towards them.

If you want to feel empowered and to have things come to you naturally, force is not the answer. Force is about trying to make things happen, trying to make people do what you want them to do. The true power of empowerment is getting people to come towards you: not forcing them to do your bidding, not pushing them to do things that go against who they are as individuals, but joining forces with you for the common good.

Force is driven by ego, pride, and fear—elements I have often seen in many leaders I've worked with.

Think about it. Ego says, "I'm really good at this. I can do this. Look at how successful I am. *Me, me, me. I, I, I.*" Many of you reading this book might not think of yourself as an egotistical person. However, if you are governed by fear, that is your ego talking. I can assure you that someone reading these words right now has made leadership decisions out of fear, pride, or ego. *What if I fail the people I'm leading? What if I fail my organization? What if I lose my job? What if I'm not successful?* When ego or lower-level consciousness takes over, we start to lead from a place of force—and things devolve from there. Suddenly, all the things we fear start happening. That ties into the Universal Principles of Abundance and Choice.

Being an empowered, power-driven leader is the exact opposite. It's *never* about fear. It's about reason, acceptance, and open-mindedness. How many leaders have you worked with who take a "my way or the highway" approach? That's an egotistical leader—a leader coming from a place of force, right? A truly empowered leader seeks input, is inclusive, and leads with principles and generosity.

We've had a great opportunity to explore how consciousness affects leaders. We've learned a lot about becoming empowered in our own right. Now, let's delve into the value of empowering our employees and teams.

Studies show that the more empowered people feel, the more satisfied they are with their jobs.[1] [2] The more people like and trust their leaders, the more they value empowerment. A study conducted by DDI some years ago found that 58% of employees surveyed quit their jobs because of their leader or boss. Let me repeat that: they quit their jobs because they didn't like their boss. That's something to think about.

Many of us have been told not to take it personally when someone quits. "The person isn't quitting you; they're just quitting the job—it happens. Don't take it personally; it's just business." That might have been true 20 years ago, but these research studies are now saying that if people don't feel job satisfaction or don't like their boss, 58% of them are quitting because of *you*. In today's world, where it's harder and harder to find great employees, you

1. Lee, A., Willis, S., Tien, A.W. (2018, March 2). When empowering employees works and when it doesn't. *Harvard Business Review*.

2. Weir, K. (13AD). Article in american psychological association, more than job satisfaction - psychologists are discovering what makes work meaningful - and how to create value in any job. *American Psychological Association*, 44(11).

can't afford for that to happen, can you? More importantly, do you want that to happen?

The more empowered people feel, the more committed they become to your company. The more committed they are to your company, the more likely they are to stay. So, we've established that empowerment increases job satisfaction, and it also increases their commitment to your company. There's another factor, which we'll cover in Chapter 7 on the **Universal Principle of Motivation**: Empowerment also increases employee motivation. Many leaders I work with say, "I just don't know how to motivate my team. I've tried everything, and nothing seems to work."

Well, let's take a closer look at empowerment.

How empowered is your team? The more empowered they feel, the more likely they are to take the initiative.

That's a common complaint I hear, "They just do their job and nothing more." That's what we're now calling "quiet quitting." In some companies, where performance is measured by task completion, employees are only doing the bare minimum to meet the expectations. Why would anyone want to perform tasks that aren't being measured? There's no reward or value in that. Is that what you want for your team? Or do you want people to take initiative? Do *you* want to be the one thinking for everyone, or do you want your employees to start thinking for themselves? People who take initiative *do* think for themselves, and consider the impact of their actions on the company.

People who feel empowered engage in problem-solving. I know that's another big complaint from leaders: "I have to think of everything. I have to solve everyone's problems."

Well, if you're solving all the problems, then guess what? You're not really empowering your employees to make decisions or problem-solve. As I mentioned before, the more empowered they feel, the more they contribute to the success of your organization or company. In today's complex and competitive world, wouldn't you want everyone on your team to contribute as much as possible to achieving successful results?

Of course, you would.

So, let's talk about mastery and how we help our employees gain the mastery needed to become fully empowered. Another expert on the subject of mastery, whom I studied extensively during my doctoral work, is Albert Bandura.

Bandura was one of the primary researchers who discussed and conducted studies on what we call self-efficacy. What is self-efficacy? It's an individual's belief in their mastery of something or their ability to succeed in a certain situation. The more people believe in their ability, the more likely they are to take on new or different tasks related to that ability. Research has now determined that this self-efficacy, or belief in one's ability to succeed, is closely related to empowerment.

Let me state that again.

Self-efficacy—an individual's belief in their ability to succeed—is closely related to feeling empowered. So, how do you foster that? That's the question. A lot of it has to do with learning and development. People today want the opportunity to learn and grow within their jobs and within the organization.

This learning and development foster mastery or self-efficacy. My question to you as a leader is: What kind of learning and development programs do you have for your team? I know that some of you give people money to take courses, or perhaps you provide some training—although, yuck, that's like teaching your dog to sit. You might be wondering why I might make that statement. Training in most business scenarios has become a version of school. You are told what to do, and then you practice what you have been instructed to do... just like teaching your dog to sit. However, learning and development for adults is best facilitated by taking a problem and working through it to find the best results. Adults learn best by problem-solving, which really is all about learning and the development of a skill. Adults utilize previous experiences to help them learn and relate to new information. In addition, adults need to know how what they are learning will help them achieve their goals. None of this occurs in most training experiences and certainly not in training your dog to sit (New England Institute of Technology). So my question is: *How do they really learn and develop on your team?*

To me, learning and development are about giving people power. It's about fostering their ability to reason. It's about their capacity to accept and work with others. It's about open-mindedness and personal growth. One of the things I've noticed in most of the leaders I work with is that they struggle with the concept of empowerment.

Here's why: I was working with a leader, Randy, and we were discussing this very topic. Randy said, "You know, I appreciate what you're saying. I know I should develop people more. I should help them learn how to do these things. But I've got to tell you, I have a super busy life. I have so many things piled on my desk that some tasks are just easier if I do them myself. Teaching somebody how to do them takes way more time than I can spare."

Now, reading this and looking at it from 30,000 feet, since you're not emotionally attached to Randy's situation, you might be laughing and thinking, *Well, Randy, you're so busy because you won't teach anyone how to do anything! You won't help them learn or develop as individuals.* And although you can see this from a distance, my question is: How often are you doing this with the people in your own organization? How many times as a leader have you said, "I'll just do it myself because I need it done right, and it'll take too long to teach someone else or correct their mistakes?"

What you're doing in these situations is leading from ego, not from empowerment. You're afraid of failure, and you're egotistical enough to believe that nobody can do the task better than you. You're driven by pride—thinking, "This work reflects on me, and if someone else doesn't do it right, it will reflect poorly on me."

That's not empowerment. So, if I want to create a mastery experience for my team, I have to help them complete tasks and challenges to gain mastery. In Randy's situation, he was complaining that he didn't have the time. What we did was reevaluate Randy's time.

We found a way to create time. How? By focusing on two employees rather than his entire team of ten. We identified two people he believed had the greatest potential to succeed and showed interest in taking on new challenges. These individuals would feel more satisfied in their roles if they had the opportunity to take on more responsibilities. We developed a learning and development program for these two people centered on two specific areas Randy needed to delegate. Did it take some time? Yes, it took about 30 days for them to get up to speed, and Randy could have completed the tasks in 30 minutes. However, after those 30 days, these two employees actually did the tasks better than Randy did. He also noticed a major change in their attitudes: they came to work happier, helped their coworkers, and showed a higher level of commitment to their jobs. It was clear they were more motivated to perform well.

Why?

Because Randy had taken the time to help them gain mastery, allowing them to learn and develop into empowered individuals on his team.

Empowered people are also involved in decision-making. How many of you, as leaders, make decisions without consulting anyone on your team? I know a lot of leaders who are frustrated because their own leaders don't involve them in the decision-making process. But I ask you: Do you allow people on your team to be involved in decision-making?

Why is involvement in decision-making so empowering?

Because when people help make decisions, they become invested in those decisions and their outcomes. Here's a little hint: This involvement and investment in the outcome changes their commitment to the process!

Another key aspect of empowerment is that it allows people to pursue opportunities that align with their personal goals. As we discussed earlier, in the context of the Universal Principle of Alignment, aligning with your employees' goals helps them grow, learn, develop and ultimately creates empowerment. This fosters a sense of mastery and belonging.

When you truly empower your people and delegate effectively, you are giving them power. And remember, power is far more effective than force. When they feel they have power, they work with you.

When they feel they are being forced into something, they work against you. What I want you to understand is that if you do not delegate and don't allow others to make decisions within your team, then you, personally, have no power. As I mentioned before, when you operate out of ego, pride, or fear, there is no way *you* can be empowered.

The action plan I suggest for this chapter is to identify one person on your team whom you would like to help become more masterful and build more self-efficacy in relation to their role. Detail the learning and development opportunities you can provide to help them become more skilled, and outline tasks you can delegate that will empower them while also empowering you.

You can choose to lead and live in a world centered on the ego or in a world that's eco-centric—focused on the world around you. To be an empowered, successful, and masterful leader, you must live in the *eco*-centric world, not the *ego*-centric one.

ACTION PLAN

Person selected to develop_____

Task(s) to be developed

_____
_____
_____
_____
_____
_____

Learning and Development Opportunities to
Help Them Gain Mastery

_____
_____
_____
_____
_____
_____
_____
_____
_____
_____
_____
_____
_____
_____
_____
_____

SEVEN

THE UNIVERSAL PRINCIPLE OF MOTIVATION

want to start with the definition of motivation because I think it's highly misunderstood. Motivation is essentially someone's willingness to do something. I heard something interesting on a podcast recently where the host said that everyone is motivated. Motivation is already present in every person. Okay, great—everyone is motivated. But as leaders, we often get frustrated when people on our team aren't motivated to do what we're asking of them.

So, let's explore the **Universal Principle of Motivation**. This principle says that when an individual has an unsatisfied need, tension is created. That tension generates the "motivation" to act in order to satisfy the need. If we, as leaders, understand that motivation already exists in everyone and isn't something we have to create, and we also understand that each individual has a need they're trying to satisfy, then we can amplify motivation by helping the person see how we can help them meet that need and reduce the tension they feel.

We want to help them satisfy that need.

Of course, we do. But many of the leaders I've worked with

have a common misunderstanding: they assume everyone they lead has the same needs that they, as leaders, have. Not true. That means not everyone is motivated by the same things you are! Let that sink in for a moment: Not everyone's motivation is the same as yours. This is one of the biggest mistakes a leader can make, assuming *This would motivate me. Why isn't it motivating them?*

Let me share a story about my client, Jennifer, and how this misconception was affecting her and her team. Jennifer had taken over a team of 20 people. This team was underperforming, and she needed to turn things around. She thought the best approach was to treat the team the way *she* would want to be treated. Jennifer decided to use principles that would motivate her.

She treated them with kindness.

She treated them as experts in their field. She said, "I'm not going to micromanage you." She wanted to give them the autonomy she would expect as a professional.

Here's the first issue with misidentifying motivation: Jennifer is a Gen Xer—someone who grew up having to figure things out and who values autonomy and being recognized as an expert and professional. Jennifer valued high performance, both in herself and others, and couldn't believe that simply giving everyone the tools they needed to succeed wasn't enough motivation.

Unfortunately for Jennifer, most of her team members were in their mid-20s—Generation Z. They didn't share her values or experiences. They didn't have the same experience or time in the business. So, treating them as though they were in their mid-40s with 15 to 20 years of experience when they were actually in their mid-20s with two to three years of experience created a disconnect. They had a very different value system than she did, and that's why Jennifer was struggling to motivate her team.

When I worked with Jennifer, the first thing we did was examine the generational differences between her and her team, as well as the personality differences. We knew that identifying these differences was the first step. I wanted Jennifer to recognize that if these individuals didn't share her personality profile or her values, there would naturally be a disconnect in motivation.

The second issue with motivation is the misconception that *you* can motivate someone. Earlier, I said we can amplify a person's existing motivation—but we cannot create it. That was Jennifer's mistake. She thought she could do something to motivate her team. Unfortunately, that's not how it works. In fact, most leaders I talk to have the same misconception. You wouldn't believe the perplexed looks I get when they say, "Deb, I need you to help me motivate my team," and I respond, "Well, that's not possible."

They immediately ask what I mean and are quick to insist that something *can* be done. But it's not that simple. So, aside from hearing that everyone is already motivated on some level, you may be wondering where this principle of motivation comes from and what I'm getting at. It comes from a psychological theory called Self-Determination Theory, developed by Deci and Ryan.[1] They determined that there are two types of motivation: intrinsic and extrinsic. Intrinsic motivation comes from within, and extrinsic motivation comes from external factors.

When individuals are intrinsically motivated, they engage in activities because they are inherently interested in or enjoy those activities. When they are extrinsically motivated, they are driven by an external reward.

An external reward isn't limited to tangible things. It's more than just money. While an extrinsic motivator could be a title, more money, or an award, it could also be the need to feel accomplished. It could also be the need to be seen by others as successful or to achieve a certain goal because of how others perceive it. For example, one of my extrinsic motivators in becoming the first female president of the Dallas Home Builders Association wasn't purely

---

1. Ryan, R., & Deci, E. (n.d.). Self-determination theory and the facilitation of intrinsic motivation, social development and well-being. January 2000. American Psychologist. https://selfdeterminationtheory.org/SDT/documents/2000_RyanDeci_SDT.pdf.

intrinsic—it was an extrinsic motivator. I wanted my dad to recognize my achievement in an industry he had spent his life in.

An important point to note is that many times, the individual isn't propelled by a passion for the goal itself, but by the need to fulfill something deeper.

Intrinsic motivators are driven by passion. It's all about doing something for the enjoyment and fulfillment you get from the task. One of my intrinsic motivators is the love of helping people succeed. I love watching them soar, excelling in ways they never thought possible. I do it because I love what I do. I do it because I have a passion for it. So, can you see how intrinsic and extrinsic motivators differ?

Now, I get asked a lot of questions about reward-based motivators, so let's address this upfront. People often ask, "Can't I just reward people extrinsically, give them what they want, and then get what I want?" The thing is, Deci and Ryan, along with other researchers on motivation, have shown that external rewards are short-term in nature.

For example, I had a client with a sales team. The client wanted to save incentive money, and to this end, they offered their salespeople the opportunity to share anything that was saved. So if the incentive was $10,000 and the salesperson only gave the customer $5,000, the company agreed to give the salesperson $2,500 of the $5,000 saved, and the company got the other half. My client was so excited about the idea and asked if I thought it was great. Unfortunately, I had to rain on their parade and suggest it wouldn't get the results they were hoping for. They disagreed, convinced that their team would be motivated to save money and, in return, make more money. So, since there was no harm in trying, we moved forward with the plan.

Guess what happened?

It only worked for people who were motivated by money. For those who weren't motivated by money—those who prioritized making clients happy or who found the negotiation process tedious

—guess what? They didn't save any more or any less than they had before. Even if they stood to gain a share, they weren't motivated to save for the company. Money wasn't a motivator for them.

I'll give you another example of how extrinsic motivators can have a negative effect. I've worked in an industry where people received bonuses for completing a project within a certain time frame. This bonus program began during a time when it was hard to meet deadlines. So, they started offering completion bonuses. Bonuses like that are *still* paid in this industry today, almost 20 years later. Why? Because the bonus shifted from being a reward to being seen as part of the compensation package. When extrinsic rewards are used inappropriately, they can change from rewards to expectations.

Many times, extrinsic reward is used as a negative force for motivation. For example, if you don't meet your sales goal, you'll lose your job. That's an external motivator, the proverbial stick as the counterpart to the carrot: "Hit your goal, or else." Sometimes, that works, but other times, people just give up and stop caring. Where's the heightened interest in getting somewhere?

Truly, when we work with intrinsic motivators—those that engage people in activities because they are inherently interested or enjoy them—that's when we see a real difference. So, what are some of these motivators that drive people to engage in activities for the sheer interest and joy of it? One would be autonomy—the ability to work independently. Another is competence, or self-efficacy—the belief in one's ability to achieve mastery. When people feel they have achieved some level of mastery, they feel more confident, more self-assured, and more optimistic about their future.

Now, let's discuss something you may not have considered as related to motivation: the values and biases we all hold. As we've mentioned, everyone has values and biases based on their background. The generation in which someone grew up is a huge factor in understanding their motivations. Many of you are leading teams composed of multiple generations. So, let's break down these different generations and look at how their biases and values can affect their motivations.

Let's start with the oldest generation and work our way to the youngest. Our first group is the Baby Boomers, people born between 1946 and 1964. I happen to be a Baby Boomer myself. We were taught by our parents to be loyal to our employers and hardworking. My dad used to tell me, "Show up before you're supposed to start, stay late, do your job, and do it to the best of your ability—you'll always be recognized for your efforts." Unfortunately, my dad was a little wrong about that. What happened when I followed his advice in my career? I just got more to do. But think about the values instilled in us. Since we were taught to be loyal to our employers and hardworking, what kinds of motivators are likely to inspire us? Things like loyalty, mentoring, helping others succeed, and recognition for a job well done are intrinsically motivating to us.

We also need to understand that our actions can be motivators. How we communicate with others, for example, can act as a motivator. I'll give you an example. My husband, who is in his early 70s and also a Baby Boomer, is very proud of the fact that he doesn't text. We had a situation with a Millennial family member who prefers texting as their main form of communication. The Millennial reached out to me via text and said, "I don't like talking on the phone, and Steve doesn't want to text, so please wish him a happy birthday for me." Now, while that seems humorous, it illustrates something important. If these two individuals were working together, one would prefer to communicate via text, while the other would prefer a phone call or face-to-face meeting. How motivated would either of them be if they continued to pursue their own communication style without adapting to the other? Let's use my husband, Steve, as an example. How many people would be motivated to work with someone who doesn't care about their preferred communication method?

I'm just thinking they probably wouldn't be very motivated,

right? They wouldn't feel engaged because their engagement looks different from my husband's engagement.

Now let's talk about Generation Xers,[2] who were born between 1965 and 1984. They had Baby Boomers as parents, and they learned a lot about loyalty, or the lack of it, from their parents' experiences. They saw their parents, who were loyal employees, get laid off, and as a result, they learned that organizations aren't loyal.

Since many Generation Xers spent a lot of time at home alone— either in a one-parent household or because both parents worked— they were forced to become self-sufficient. So, what do you think motivates a Generation Xer? Self-sufficiency, right? The ability to figure things out themselves because no one was there to teach them. They were the original latchkey kids. Many make career changes to get ahead because they saw their parents stagnate in jobs or get laid off. For them, to get more pay or a better title, they believe they need to move on to a different job.

Many Generation Xers, because they were left on their own, had to find information, learn how to do things, or find a community to support them. Not only did they gain the information and support they needed, but they also learned to embrace social diversity in ways their parents never did.

These individuals, having been raised by two working parents or a single parent, often made the decision that when they became parents, they would leave their jobs to create the ideal family environment. So, many times, Generation Xers are motivated by short-term monetary gains to achieve financial security when one parent wants to stay home to raise the family.

So what motivates a Gen Xer? As I said, it's autonomy versus loyalty, right? It's the ability to switch jobs rather than staying in the same job, working hard, and waiting to be recognized. It's

---

2. Tulgan, B. (2000). *Managing Generation X: How to Bring Out the Best in Young Talent.* W.W. Norton.

about making more money to achieve financial security faster, or maybe even staying employed while working from home.

Now let's move on to Generation Y, or the Millennials, born between 1985 and 2000. This generation is interesting because their motivators are varied. Some were raised by Baby Boomers with Baby Boomer values, while others were raised by Gen Xers, who have very different values.

Can you already see why people in your organization may react differently to corporate policy, motivation strategies, or you as a leader? It goes back to my client, Jennifer, who tried to motivate her team based on what motivated her. Jennifer is a Gen Xer who values autonomy.

What did she do? She tried to motivate people by giving them autonomy. She recognized them as professionals with abilities and mastery, which are things she values. Being recognized in that way engaged her in the activities she was asked to do because they became inherently interesting to her. So, as I've mentioned, the Millennial group either has values more aligned with Baby Boomers or those that align with Gen Xers.

And now, let's discuss Generation Z, born between 1997 and 2012. This generation is seeking purpose and meaning in the work-place. Going back to Jennifer—she's promoting autonomy while these employees are looking for purpose and meaning. The two don't match.

They're looking for real experiences. But with little to no experience in the job, what exactly is a "real experience?" How do they use these experiences to create meaning and purpose? Jennifer wasn't helping them with that. She was preaching a set of values that couldn't possibly resonate with her team.

Moreover, this team, composed of many Generation Zers, is seeking financial security. They want to save money, yet they find themselves in a commission-based sales job during a tremendous market shift. How can they feel financially secure in such a job?

While the Boomer generation were spenders, Generation Z is

focused on becoming financially independent. They watched their parents lose things and saw their Gen X parents struggle. If they had a Gen X parent, which many did, they likely experienced a one-income household. Yes, their mom or dad was home with them every day when they got home from school, but they probably weren't very financially independent because they were living off a single income.

Gen Xers are self-sufficient.

Now let's look at the disconnect between Gen Xers and Millennials. Even Gen Xers who raised Millennial children often struggle to work in a motivational environment with Millennials. Why? The autonomous Gen Xer doesn't understand the Millennial's need for mentorship. Gen Xers figured out how to get things done on their own, so why can't Millennials do the same? Can you now see why trying to lead or motivate using methods that would work for you might not be working for others?

Lastly, I want to talk about the role of the environment—both physical and non-physical—in motivation. The study I mentioned earlier provides a comprehensive analysis. But if you don't have the time or inclination to read a lot of research, I'll share a great hack.

You can start using this hack in the interview process or with anyone who works with you right now. Ask them two specific questions. Here's the first one: "Tell me about a job you were so excited about, one you found so satisfying that you could barely contain yourself from getting to work early. Tell me about the environment that existed. What did your leader do to help you feel this way?" Guess what? They just defined the environment in which they feel engaged and interested.

Now, if your employee is too young to have had many other jobs, ask them about a professor in college or a teacher in school. That will give you the same information.

The second question to ask is, "Tell me about a time when you disliked your job so much that you hated Sunday evenings because it meant you had to go back to work on Monday. You just couldn't wait to take your vacation. If you didn't feel well, you called in sick because who cares?" Have them describe that environment. Ask them to tell you about their boss or leader in that environment.

Now you know what a demotivating, unengaging, and inherently uninteresting environment looks like to this person. They've told you, so the guesswork is gone. The simpler you can make it, the easier it becomes.

The action plan I want you to undertake in this chapter is to think about one employee you'd like to help feel more engaged and inherently interested in what they do every day. This could be by helping them become more autonomous, more competent, more connected—whatever you think is needed.

The second step is to sit down and use the two-pronged question approach. Have that conversation to find out what's going on in their mind. Learn exactly what kind of environment engages and interests them, and what kind of environment disengages and disinterests them. Then create a plan to make that happen for that employee.

In this chapter, we've focused on unsatisfied needs, the tension that creates, and the difficulties that arise when people are disengaged and unmotivated.

When you change your approach, determine their needs, and learn what engages and interests them in their job, you can create an environment where your team becomes absolutely, positively engaged, motivated, and excited to make a difference. And when they start making a difference in your organization and for the people you serve, you'll have made a lasting impact as a leader in their lives—one they will never forget.

ACTION PLAN

Pick an employee _____

Findings from a conversation about motivational environments

_____

_____

_____

_____

_____

_____

_____

How you can integrate those factors into their environment

_____

_____

_____

_____

_____

_____

_____

What generation do they belong to _____

What do they value

_____

_____

_____

_____

_____

_____

_____

How you can incorporate those values into how you work together

_____

_____

_____

_____

_____

_____

_____

_____

_____

EIGHT

THE UNIVERSAL PRINCIPLE
OF ACTION

What is the definition of action in and of itself? Well, dictionaries say that it's really the process of doing something to achieve an aim or simply get something done.

If we look at the word "act" itself, what does it mean? It refers to behaving in a specified way. Now, how does all of that relate to the **Universal Principle of Action**, and what is that? The Universal Principle of Action states that if we take deliberate action—notice the word deliberate, meaning planned and strategic—on behalf of the people we want to either shift, develop, or help grow. The universe takes this as a sign of readiness and then brings you the results you can handle. Let's break that down.

When we take deliberate action, it means an intentional, strategic action. This action is taken on behalf of someone—whether we're trying to shift their perspective, develop them as a leader, or help them grow in their own right.

According to this principle, the universe takes our deliberate action as a signal that we are ready. In response, it brings us results, but here's the key: It brings you the results you can handle. I think that's where many leaders struggle. We often act on the basis of the reaction we want, but what I've learned from experience is that the universe gives us what we can handle—not necessarily the reaction we expect. Interestingly, author Jennifer Longmore said, "Knowledge is action," and I believe she's right. Because if we look at this universal principle, we must understand where people are in their journey. We need to know how to strategically help them, be clear on our intentions, and understand how they need to develop and how *they* want to grow.

A crucial aspect of the Universal Principle of Action is knowledge. Without knowledge, action is impossible to take.

As leaders, our gifts and talents only become real when we bring them to life through action. Until we take action, our talents are just possibilities or dreams.

Another important aspect of the Universal Principle of Action is the concept of inaction. Not taking action is an action in itself. Too often, I see leaders say, "I'm just going to let this play out," or, "I'll sit back and see what happens." But how is that intentional? How does that tell the universe we're ready to move forward, help people grow, or be deliberate in our leadership?

When we don't take action and allow others to act for us, what happens? Nine times out of 10, we're not happy with the actions they take. I also believe many of us fear taking action because we fear a bad result or getting it wrong. Of course, we don't want to be wrong—especially as Baby Boomers, for whom failure is often seen as the ultimate setback. Yet, for Millennials, Zoomers, and Generation Xers, failure is often viewed as a learning opportunity. Leaning into failure is talked about a lot these days, and while we might say failure helps us grow, I'm not sure we always believe it deep down.

How many failures did Einstein endure before developing the theory of relativity? How many times did Edison fail before inventing the light bulb? We quote these examples, but many of us still have a deep fear of bad results or disappointing those we lead.

The **Universal Principle of Abundance**, which we've discussed before, teaches us that we get more of what we focus on. Remember that? Whatever we think about, we attract more of. That's the rule of abundance. You can have abundance in anything. We often associate abundance with good things, but an abundance of bad things also exists. You've heard people say, "If it weren't for bad luck, I'd have no luck at all." That's where they are abundant—in bad luck. In the Universal Principle of Action, we understand that whatever we focus on and act on, we will get more of it. If we choose to do nothing, we'll get an abundance of other people's actions controlling our lives.

If we take abundant, deliberate, and intentional action for the good of others, what do you think will happen? More great, intentional good for others. You'll see them grow, prosper, and succeed.

This concept of action is also closely tied to the **Universal Principle of Focus**, which we've already discussed. What we focus on is where our energy goes. So, if we review the actions we can take and decide to act deliberately with great intention, focusing on developing people and fostering growth, the reactions we get will reflect that. If our actions are rooted in positive intentions, we will get more of the same. But when we fear taking action because we worry about the outcome, we limit the positive potential of our actions.

What if it's wrong? What if it doesn't work out right? If you hold a positive intention, a positive thought, or a positive choice, might you not get a positive outcome? In my life, I can tell you, I absolutely have. Now, let's take action and apply this Universal Principle of Action to something so many leaders have talked to me about—the idea of a difficult conversation. In fact, I am frequently asked to either speak or teach about having difficult conversations.

But the first place I start is by asking, "How did this conversation become difficult?" I would say it's related to action or inaction, and that's an important point. If we look at all of the other things we do as leaders, we can often avoid difficult conversations altogether.

If we've taken the Universal Principle of Action and acted on setting performance goals to help people get where they want to go, will we get a negative reaction, or will we get a different one? I start with an action. I act on goal-setting with someone to help them achieve the results they want, which in turn benefits everyone. If I've taken action on goal-setting and actively discussed accountability, as we've covered in other chapters, then what will we get?

The action of maintaining accountability, of helping people remain accountable based on what they told you they needed to do to achieve their goals, will inevitably lead to a different result than having a difficult conversation. When we do goal-setting, establish performance goals, and have accountability conversations, we help people obtain the goals they want to achieve—not the goals we want to achieve. Remember that. You never succeed as a leader by making others work toward your goals. It's about helping others attain theirs. When we push our own goals, we're taking action that's not in alignment with our employees.

If our actions aren't aligned with where people want to go, why are we shocked when we get a negative result by asking people to match the goals of the corporation? This is where the Universal Principle of Action applies.

It starts in performance conversations. It starts with goal-setting. That's a really important thing to remember. Having that conversation upfront can prevent the need for a difficult conversation later. Now, I realize that many of you are just reading this book for the first time, and you're thinking, *Oh gosh, I haven't implemented all of that yet. I'm just starting to.* So, how do you handle a difficult conversation that's already arisen because you didn't implement these things earlier?

First, take action, set the alignment, and establish that this is going to be a positive experience for the person you lead, as well as for yourself. The fact that we're calling it a difficult conversation suggests we already expect it to be hard and that the result is likely going to be negative. But if I enter the conversation with positive thoughts about how it can be aligned with the person's goals and how it can help them grow and develop, then maybe the conversation will be all good.

So why do people fear these conversations? A lot of our hesitation stems from fear. Research gives us a couple of reasons.

First, we fear hurting the relationship. Maybe we haven't taken action to correct something early on because we were afraid of damaging the relationship. Unfortunately, our earlier inaction in not addressing the issue has actually put the relationship at greater risk. Now that we've let things go for so long, how do we maintain a good relationship with this person?

If we want to keep the relationship strong, we need to ask ourselves: *Isn't this person wondering how much you really like and respect me if you didn't tell me earlier that there was an issue?* That's a valid point.

The second fear is that we're uncomfortable with conflict. Where our focus goes, our energy flows. So, if we focus on conflict, what are we going to get? Conflict. And we'll get an abundance of it. We're also worried that the other person will become angry. Yet the Universal Principle of Action tells us that if we're deliberate and strategic in our approach and do it in the interest of the person's growth and development, why would they become angry? Many times, I've been afraid of saying something the wrong way or saying the wrong thing. I believe that often ties back to inaction.

We avoid having conversations about behaviors we don't agree with. We don't want to deal with complaints from other employees about someone, so we tell ourselves, *I'm too busy right now. I'll address it tomorrow.* Many of us do this at home with our children. What happens then is our emotions build up until we reach a breaking point. That's when we should fear saying the wrong thing or reacting poorly because now we're acting not strategically but out of irritation and anger.

That, of course, relates to the Principle of Alignment. We're not in alignment with the person we're talking to. Sometimes, it's because we fear being wrong or not knowing enough. And that, especially if we say something wrong during a conversation because we didn't clearly understand, implies we're not good listeners. We are not actively listening. If any of you have ever studied active listening, you'll know that it requires being fully present in the *now*. An active listener isn't already solving the problem while someone is talking to them. Sometimes, conversations become difficult because we're not taking the action of being a good listener.

And then there's the fear of losing emotional control. Have you ever been in a situation where you had to talk with someone, and they began crying? I can tell you this has happened to me on more than one occasion in my career. As a woman leader, I often see this happening with men. These men were so frustrated with the situation that the only thing they could do was cry. That certainly says it all. I had waited *way* too long to have the conversation!

That taught me right then and there that if I had to talk to someone and they were this frustrated during the conversation, I had not done a good job as the leader I wanted to be because I hadn't taken action early enough. I hadn't taken the actions necessary to allow that person to change course. I had put that person in a position where all they could do was listen to a list of things they had done wrong and how they needed to correct them instead of having conversations along the way that would have helped me understand why they handled the situation the way they did. These conversations could have uncovered aspects of their personal life that might explain why they were late to work or distracted on the job. It does not excuse everything, but many times, simply understanding what someone is going through helps us make sense of their actions. Correct? These different fears certainly affect our ability or willingness to take action.

But let's continue to discuss the difficult conversation. We have different choices we can make about how to approach these conversations. Remember we discussed the **Universal Principle of Choice**? What choices can we make in these types of conversations, and what usually happens?

Here are some choices we can make, and here are some actions we can take. The first, which I've spent a lot of time discussing, is choosing avoidance. Avoiding the conversation altogether is, in itself, an action. Then, we have the choice to take action by simply giving in. Many of us have done that as leaders. We're busy; we've heard it all before, and we just don't want to deal with it today. So what action do we take? We give in, thinking, *It's not that important anyway, so I'll just let them have it their way.* But we know this action doesn't usually get us great results because it isn't rooted in strategy or a deliberate effort to help them grow. Instead, this action is based on avoiding the problem because we don't want to deal with it. Again, we are not in alignment.

The third option is being passive-aggressive. We've all met people like this. I can tell you, I was once married to a person like that—it's not fun. On the surface, they act as though everything is great, but then, after you've left the office, they talk negatively about you to their coworkers. But leaders can do this too. That's what leads to passive-aggressive employees.

What about us as passive-aggressive leaders? We go in and say we want to help someone change and grow, but then we walk out of the office and complain about them to other employees. Unfortunately, I see that a lot in leadership.

Many women take this style of leadership. They make things look good on the surface, but then walk around the employee and stab them in the back. Or they use someone else to try to convey the difficult message. That never works. Take ownership of your actions.

Another action is to bully. There are many leaders, and maybe some of you reading this book have been that leader in the past, who say, "It's my way or the highway." That's the action of a bully. It's, "I don't care about your problems, I don't care about your

goals, I only care about what I want, and I'll bully you into it."
Remember the story I told about my boss coming in and telling me
to fire someone? He bullied me. His action was to intimidate me—if
I didn't want to do it, he would find someone else to fire me.

Another action is compromise, right? Now, many of you are
probably thinking, *Isn't that a good action—to compromise?* It can be,
but it also has its downsides. Compromise says, "I'll have to give
something up, and you'll have to give something up, too." That's
Negotiation 101. But do we really want to negotiate on someone's
behalf? Do we really want to negotiate their ability to grow and
develop? Personally, I don't. My job as a leader is to see things in
people that they may not even see in themselves.

So that leads us to the next action, which is really the best
action: to problem-solve and come to a decision together. That's not
necessarily a compromise. It's about leading them to certain conclu-
sions where we can help them develop and see how they can grow.
What is the action we're now taking? I think this is a really important point: take the action of being judgment-free. Sometimes we let
our emotions build up so much when we have to have these
conversations that we strategically prep for every eventuality. We
try to figure out how it's really going to go—do they really trust
me?

Unfortunately, I had to go through this with my mother in a
recent family situation that was really difficult for her. My brother
and I found ourselves judging the other person involved, making
assumptions about their intentions and actions. And you know
what we found out at the end of the day?

Well, first, I'll step back and say that we both had a conversation
to release our judgments and assumptions. We knew it was going
to be a difficult conversation. This situation involved mediation,
and it was a long day.

But at the end of the day, because we released our judgments
and assumptions, things turned out far better and far less stressful
for my mother than we had possibly imagined. So, I'm asking you

as a leader: When you have to have these conversations, don't judge, don't make assumptions, and don't prepare for every possible outcome. Nine times out of ten, you're going to be wrong. How many times have you thought, *Oh my gosh, this is going to be horrible,* only to find out it was never nearly as bad as you thought?

Another point I want to address about difficult conversations is the use of self-discovery. What does that mean? It requires you to learn about the other person. It requires you to ask questions of them—not to come in guns blazing. It also involves, as I mentioned earlier regarding compromises, helping the other person discover something about themselves. The more people discover about themselves, the more willing they are to change their behavior. Self-discovery leads to the need for change, not just because you told them to. I think that is important for us as leaders to remember.

The last thing I would like to say about difficult conversations and the actions we take is that results are neither good nor bad. No matter what happens when you take action—whether it's in a difficult conversation or any action as a leader—results are neither good nor bad. It's the value you assign to them that creates the problem.

Think about that for a minute.

Something happens, and we say, "Oh, that was a bad day." You assigned the value that it was a bad day, which now makes the day a problem. Were the results themselves good or bad? No, they just *were*. The more we can stop assigning a value to results, the less it becomes a problem for us. It's very much like what I experienced when creating my research study for my doctorate. The first thing they teach you is that you want to come up with a hypothesis for the research study you're going to undertake. The results you get either prove your hypothesis, disprove it, or tell you nothing at all.

Now, the problem with most research is that we have bias, which we've discussed before, and that bias relates to the values we assign. Many times in research, the researcher has a bias about what they want to happen, and they structure their hypothesis in such a way that they get the desired outcome.

Actions are like this, too. They either prove something, disprove something, or tell us nothing at all.

As leaders, we must be courageous. I've just talked about all the fears we have, but courage says, "I will act in the face of all my fears. I will act regardless of them."

I will act in accordance with the alignment of others. I will act with focus on what I want to cultivate in this person. I will act in abundance—the abundance of good things and good opportunities for this person.

The action plan I would ask you to undertake is to pick an issue or challenge you're currently facing with someone. Create positive intentions for change. Then, based on this universal principle of action, ask yourself: *What are my intentions? What is my strategy to help this individual develop and grow?* Outline your steps of action and base them on all the principles we have discussed in this book.

Hopefully, through this chapter, you've learned one thing: Action is a principle. When you take action, it tells the universe you are ready for it to provide what you are ready to undertake. And that is a pretty powerful feeling.

ACTION PLAN

Person I want to have a conversation with _____

My intentions for change are

_____

_____

_____

_____

_____

_____

My strategies to help this person grow are

_____
_____
_____
_____
_____
_____
_____
_____
_____
_____

My action steps are

_____
_____
_____
_____
_____
_____
_____
_____
_____

CONCLUSION

As I conclude this book, I want to leave you with one last tip. It could be a universal principle, but I'm not going to call it that. This is something I've learned that has helped me immensely and will help you on your leadership journey, too: gratitude. I know—overstated, overused, and everyone talks about it.

And yet, I can tell you that if you can embrace gratitude on this leadership journey, it will forever change your life. Now, what I want to focus on is what gratitude really looks like in your day and how it can positively change your day before you even leave the house. The first thing to know is that how you start your day affects everything about your day. I heard a talk by Louise Hay and Wayne Dyer, and they explained how valuable the first 17 seconds of your day are.

Think about that—the first 17 seconds that shape your day. What does that mean? Their contention was that when you first wake up, you're coming out of delta and theta brain states.

Theta wavelength is where we're easily programmed—where our brains function during sleep, somewhere between theta and delta wavelengths. As we wake up, we're starting to come out of that theta state. This is when your subconscious brain is most easily programmed. That's why the first 17 seconds before you leave the subconscious and transition into consciousness allow you to program your brain. All you need to do in those first 17 seconds, when you start to realize you've come out of sleep and are waking up, is ask yourself, *What am I thankful for?* You don't have to say it out loud; you don't have to shout it to the world—just say it to yourself.

Thank you. Thank you. For example, for me, my first "thank you" every day is for life. My second "thank you" is for my husband. My third "thank you" is for good health, and it goes on from there. It's not hard, it's not complicated, and I guarantee every one of you, no matter where you are in life, can find something to be thankful for. When you do this, you've now primed your subconscious to look for positive things. So even when the day is fraught with stress and overwhelm, those negative events don't seem to affect you as much as they used to. When I start my day with gratitude, guess what? None of the negative events look the same. Every situation seems easier to solve. Every stress seems to melt away when I reflect on those things I'm grateful for.

Now, if you really want to take the extra step, when you get up in the morning, write in your gratitude journal. I'm sure you've heard of it before. You don't have to spend hours writing in it—just take five minutes to jot down the things you're grateful for.

I also want you to think about finding gratitude in every situation you face as a leader. As we've discussed before, ask yourself, *Why is this happening for me?* When you look at every situation as happening *for* you, the results you face will be different.

Live with grace and acceptance to learn. Grace, when given, is always returned to you. Why not give that gratitude and grace to others? What I want you to understand is that you also need to take action on those feelings of gratitude.

It's not just about what you found interesting in this book and then putting it back on the shelf—it's about putting it all to use. I want you to take the concepts I've presented here and truly apply them to your life. Like many people, I've bought tons of books. Have you ever seen my library? Oh my gosh, people are shocked and amazed at all the books I have, and they ask, "Have you read all of them?"

And I can honestly say yes. But if you ask me, "Have you applied everything you've learned from every book you've read?" Unfortunately, the answer is no.

Some of those books were enjoyable.

Some of those books were interesting. But many of them just went back on the shelf.

In order to change, you have to take action on what we've discussed in this book. Hopefully, I've broken these concepts down in a way that makes them easy to implement.

Utilize the Action Plan section I provided in each chapter. If you find a way to implement what you've just learned, I know it will make a difference in your life. Why?

Because adults learn by solving problems, these action plans will help you solve those problems.

Another tip: Try getting up 10 minutes earlier each day.

As I've said, there's always a need and place for gratitude. For you, it might be writing in your gratitude journal or maybe just thinking about what you're thankful for. But as leaders, we get so caught up in the stress, the overwhelm, and the ringing phone that we never stop to see the beauty of the world.

We never stop to hear the silence in the early morning hours. We never stop to appreciate the beauty, uniqueness, and specialness of those we lead. I'm actually tearing up just writing these words because they speak to my heart. Every day, we have an opportunity to make a difference in someone's life as a leader. These principles won't just change your life; they'll give you the opportunity to change the lives of others.

Think about this for a minute:

You can help someone you lead change their life at work. Maybe they'll feel more empowered, happier, or more accomplished. Do you think that a less stressed, more accomplished person who feels aligned with their job and motivated to go to work will now treat their family and friends differently? Or see their life in a new way? I assure you, because I've watched it happen in my own life and in the lives of those I've taught how to lead this way, they have made these changes, bettered themselves, and helped others make these changes in their own lives.

I will always ask if the people you're leading saw that you were gone one day, would they say that having known you made their lives better in some way? My fervent hope, wish, and desire is that by reading my words and learning from my experiences, even though I may have never met you personally, I have made your life better in some way.

THANK YOU FOR READING MY BOOK!

Thank you!

DOWNLOAD YOUR FREE GIFTS

Just to say thanks for buying and reading my book, I would like to give you a free bonus gift, no strings attached!

Scan the QR Code:

SCAN ME

I appreciate your interest in my book and value your feedback
as it helps me improve future versions of this book.
I would appreciate it if you could leave your invaluable review
on Amazon.com with your feedback.
Thank you!

www.ingramcontent.com/pod-product-compliance
Lightning Source LLC
Chambersburg PA
CBHW021944190326
41519CB00009B/1132